Unconquerable Soul

One Man's Thorny Path to Freedom

A story of courage and personal triumph during fifteen years of communist imprisonment

Bret Dofek

Unconquerable Soul: One Man's Thorny Path to Freedom
A story of courage and personal triumph during
fifteen years of communist imprisonment
by Bret Dofek

Published by Bret Dofek

Editor: Melanie Mulhall, www.thatcopywriter.com

Cover and Book Design: Nick Zelinger, www.nzgraphics.com

Library of Congress Catalog Control Number: 2010908230

ISBN: 978-0-9828034-0-0

First Edition

Printed in the United States of America

Books may be purchased by contacting the author at:
bretdofek1@yahoo.com

This book is dedicated to my parents, Joseph and Stefany Dofek, to my oldest brother Joe, to my Uncle Luis, and to the many thousands of other political prisoners during the Marxist communist dictatorships of 1948-1989.

It is impossible to name all of my fellow prisoners with whom I put my life, health, and safety on the line against the inhuman behavior of the communist regime. My gratitude and admiration go out to them all; in our support for each other and the lasting friendships between all of us.

Finally, I am endlessly thankful to my wife, Vlasta (Atka), and to our children: sons, Bret and Rene, and daughter, Patty, for their love and support during the good and bad times.

CONTENTS

FOREWORD

What makes us human and what does it mean to be human? As humans, is it our nature to stretch ourselves and grow? And is the capacity to love hardwired within us? What makes one human mistreat another? Can we retain our humanity under the most dehumanizing conditions imaginable? And if so, how? What is freedom and what does it mean to be free? Is freedom free or is there a price to pay for it? Can it be lost through apathy or inattention?

These are not new questions. They are perennials. Every generation asks them and no generation has had all the answers. Perhaps there are no answers. Perhaps we must all sort these things out for ourselves.

Bret Dofek may not have been fed these questions along with his first solid food as a baby, but he came to ask them relatively early in life just the same. Because he had to. Because his life and his sanity required it of him and his own human nature posed the questions for him when he became a political prisoner at the age of nineteen.

Bret spent fifteen years in communist prisons and camps, under conditions that killed many of his peers and twisted many others, but left Bret and some of his fellow political prisoners with worldviews, philosophies, and understandings of what it means to be human that most of us can barely imagine—but can learn from.

Among the things that Bret learned is that human beings hold within themselves a spiritual nature that must be encouraged and developed if we are to become full human beings. He also learned that one of the best defenses against hatred and oppression is mental training—a process he refers to as "mental exercising"—the deliberate questioning of one's thoughts and beliefs, the vigilant purging of the negative from the interior landscape and refinement of the positive. And he learned that every human must develop the best in himself if he is to have a life of richness and integrity.

None of these learnings came easily and while some of Bret's practices will become evident during the telling of his story (practices like meditation, contemplation, prayer, and self-questioning, along with behavioral disciplines that fostered impeccability and integrity), the precise mechanics of how he managed the learning remains something of a mystery, even to Bret. You will not find a how-to book here. You will find one man's journey to freedom—and it is an inspiring tale. You will be given some breadcrumbs to lead you on the path to yourself. With luck, you will begin ask your own questions about what it means to be human.

And you will come to an understanding that freedom is not free. It is paid for through vigilance, the scrupulous development of character, and the willingness to put yourself on the line. Like Bret did. Like so many others have before him and like many heroes have since.

Is Bret a hero? I cannot imagine him ever using the word, but I believe he is. And I believe that he is a wise man whose story should be read with thoughtful consideration. Why? Because our freedom is dependent upon our awareness of what it means to be free and our humanity is dependent upon our willingness to develop ourselves as humans. And without freedom and humanity, we are shells of people instead of the powerful, positive creative forces that we can be, individually and collectively.

Above all else, this is a story about the endurance of human will and the indomitability of the human soul. May we all endure, and may we shine.

Melanie Mulhall

Author of *Living the Dream*

May, 2010

INTRODUCTION

The road to freedom can be very long, steep, and difficult. I know. I learned it over fifteen years in communist prisons and concentration camps. During those years, I realized that I risked losing more than my physical freedom. I could lose something more valuable: trust in myself, in my human nature. I could lose trust in humanity and in the meaning and purpose of life. I realized that before I could earn my spiritual freedom, my peace of mind, my stability, and my integrity, I had to call forth everything that I had in my potential, everything that was still hidden there, unused.

But before I was taken prisoner, I had no preparation to help me avoid becoming a victim and slave of the deteriorating, self-destructive tendencies within my personality. I had not learned how to develop mental stability, inner balance, and harmony or how to extend the functions of my mind to enhance my health, safety, and prosperity. To achieve that state of mind, I had to challenge everything, including my ideas about what it meant to be whole and safe, as well as what it meant to have a healthy and productive personality.

What I found, what I gained during my lengthy incarceration, surprised me. I came to the realization that there is a different world, a mostly uncharted mental and spiritual world with its own set of rules. It is a world that is known by few people, but a world that, in a very dramatic way, affects everyone's quality of our life. The mental, physical, and spiritual strength I gained in those prisons, over time, is something beyond anyone's imagination.

Our schools teach us everything but how to organize our lives to fully succeed. As parents and teachers, we fail to teach children practical lessons: how to express themselves in ways that stabilize their behavior; how to be prepared for the future; how to have bright, healthy, safe, and prosperous lives. By failing to teach them how to exercise their minds, we fail to help them expand their responses to life or expand their vision. Without that mental training, they cannot express freedom of choice, freedom in their decision making. Nor can they build common sense or understand the role of their own spirit. Without guidance, they may fail to learn that spirit is an undeniable, inseparable part of themselves.

Teaching what constitutes human nature should be a priority in their learning process. Who are they and where do they belong in this natural process of life? What are their fundamental needs? How can they be fully prepared to deal with complexities of their lives when so many things can go wrong? How can they retain their inner balance, stability, and harmony and how can they retain the harmony in their relationships with others? These are the things they need to know.

To expect that they will fully succeed in their life without practical, teachable lessons in these things is foolishness. When they are not prepared, not fully matured, and still vulnerable to the world's pressures, they will have less ability rise up to meet all that will be against them unless they have this firm foundation. Misery, apathy, anxiety, emptiness, and depression cannot come into their lives unless their weak, confused, and disoriented spirits are unable to filter, defuse, and dispose of all negatives. And if they are overcome by the negative, what will happen to their unexplored and unused potential?

If we are without clarity, if we fail to be in control of ourselves, if we lack a sense of direction, then we are vulnerable to being misled by others and vulnerable to the self-destructive tendencies within our own behavior patterns. If we allow ourselves to spin chaotically, and if we have no sense of whether the momentum and direction of that spin goes against our own human nature, against our inner balance, or against harmonious relationships with others, then we are no better than a small fish, tangled in the net, unable to free itself.

At the very least, we should be concerned for our own physical, mental, and spiritual health. We should be concerned about our over-all development. Otherwise, we might become tangled like those small fish in the net . . . and we might remain tangled for as long as we live. Unable to free ourselves from that net, we live lives of low standards, performance, expectations, and achievements. And if we fail to free ourselves from the net, we should not blame anyone but ourselves.

But most of us are not as free as we think we are.

Among the most damaging beliefs held by most people today is the belief that freedom is free, that it comes without our doing anything to deserve it. Many hold this same belief about their health, safety, and prosperity. But if we wish to achieve and maintain optimal health, we need to do more than we are traditionally accustomed to doing. It is not enough just to watch our diets or engage in physical exercise. We need to go into the depths of our human nature. There are still plenty of resources hidden, unused in our potential, that we need to bring up into the mind. To do this requires us to exercise our minds, just as we would exercise our bodies.

Those of us who live in the free world often *do* take our freedom for granted. We *do* forget that freedom must be earned. We lack the mental discipline to search the depths of our own human nature for strength and clarity of spirit. And without that mental discipline, we lack the ability to solve problems, reverse bad energy, and improve both our values and our experience. Without that mental discipline, we lose our driving power and our self-esteem. But by exercising our minds, we should be able to open fully to our inner selves, our potential, and our very souls.

Like many in this world, I grew up under the pressure of a totalitarian, despotic regime. Those who live with this kind of oppression are desperately searching for freedom. And it does not come easily. It does not come at all unless or until we gain the mental and spiritual vision to see and confront what blocks our ability to be free, healthy, and safe. And that mental and spiritual vision only comes by climbing the high hills and deep valleys of our interior lives in the natural process of self-development. Only then can we become whole. Only then will we have healthy personalities. And only then can we gain our true freedom.

There is much misery and confusion in the world. Many exist without really living, harboring feelings of emptiness, apathy, anxiety, depression and instability. But what is the cause? My own struggles, through fifteen years of incarceration within Russian prisons, taught me that the underlying cause of all human misery and suffering can be found within our inner being. Though unintentional, our misery is self-created. We become insensitive—our affects flat, our personalities shallow, and our thinking superficial. We lose our ability to care about our own lives or about society as a whole.

And in this state, we are, indeed, like fish tangled in a net. But our net is fashioned by the self-destructive elements of our own person-alities. And like those fish, tangled in a net, we are unable to break through and be free.

What can set us free? Unlike those fish tangled in a net, we have the ability to rise up and fight for our both our internal freedom and our freedom in the world. Like everything else in life, it takes enthusiasm and the desire to be the best human beings we can be. But many of us are in limbo. We wish to break through the bonds of our tangled net, but we do not know how. Worse, we have become complacent.

Unfortunately, we may lose the ability to possess the most basic of human needs—health, safety, and self-determination—if we remain numbly entangled in our net. Without exercising our minds, without challenging our assumptions and developing our spiritual muscles, we will become our own worst enemies.

It is insidious. On the football field, our opponent—our "enemy"— is visible to us. He is before our eyes and we know that his intention is to thwart us and win. Further, there are rules to the game. But when the opponent is our own confused and disoriented spirit, the "enemy" is invisible and, like an invisible opponent on the football field, he may throw us off from our inner balance and harmony. Ironically, the enemy within may, ultimately, influence us to go against our own, overall healthy development. And we do not know the rules of the game.

We must learn the rules of the game, must understand them, accept them, and learn to adjust. And just like the football player, we need to see where our weakness and vulnerability are and try to eliminate them to become stronger and more successful in the game of life. We need to be in condition to be able to break through the self-destructive tendencies within ourselves. We need to clearly see and understand the driving power, purpose, and reason for our lives and why our own lives are worth fighting for. As important, we need to clearly see and understand the opposition and why that destructive power hidden behind our confused and disoriented spirits is fighting for our destruction.

We become vulnerable when we do not have a fundamental line of positive values—inner balance, peace of mind, stability, and harmony— within us, and when we don't hold to those values. But to hold only positive values like kindness, honesty, or good intentions, does not work by itself. We may still become defenseless against the constant attack of apathy, moral indifference, and other opponents that reside both within ourselves and within society. And we may still fall prey to emptiness within our own souls.

Why? Because our old, traditional, inconsistent view on life does not have a strong, impenetrable, protective shield against the sharp edges of negative values, including the self-destructive tendencies within ourselves. It does not have the vision to understand the whole picture, the whole process of our development. It does not see the final destination of the developmental process.

Human nature *is* designed to do better. Human nature *does* have the ability to defend every aspect of health, safety, and prosperity. Our ability to defend ourselves when our personality is danger of falling apart is our power.

In the game of life, we must use our potential. It is our primary resource and we must use it wisely. Within it is breadth of vision, inner strength, ambition, enlightenment, and empowerment. But where should we focus our attention? How should we invest this natural resource? We should invest in our inner balance and stability.

Just as a house must have a good foundation if the walls, floor, and roof are to be strong and endure, so must we build our lives upon a strong foundation. When we build our foundation on the moral character that comes from rigorous self-examination and mental exercise, we can create lives of richness and quality, make full use of our potential, and develop spiritual muscle.

The world today is unstable, uncertain, and turbulent. For those whose internal processes are immature and undeveloped, who have not yet developed that moral and spiritual muscle, it can be a very dangerous place. Unless we stop and consider where we are going in this game of life and what we are really trying to achieve, we may simply continue to press forward, aiming for little more than a secure livelihood and material possessions. Even if we are trying to be useful, responsible citizens, we will have, at best, external success if we fail to develop mental and spiritual discernment.

It is important to step back and take some time for ourselves, carve out a bit of space in which we can think about how we are playing this game of life and what adjustments might be needed. This means stretching our brain muscles, recovering our sense of self, using techniques like deep relaxation, and recharging ourselves so we can strengthen our ability to play the game with vision and clarity. This is not, after all, simply a game in which the goal is to win a trophy or recognition. This is a serious fight for our lives, our souls, and every important aspect of our health, safety, prosperity and freedom.

This is a lengthy process. A game on the football field lasts only a couple of hours. But the game of life lasts our whole lives. Every new day is a new beginning with new challenges and new learning experiences. We need to have excitement and high spirits. And we must have the ability to recognize and reverse occasional lapses into lethargy and monotony.

For that, we have to put everything in our human nature in order:

- We must use our ability to exercise mentally, that is, to engage in a rigorous program of mental training. We must extend our responses beyond our habitual and unquestioned limits, broaden our vision, spread our wings of freedom, understand the inner causes of our behavior, and prevent the negative consequences of an unexamined life.
- We must explore our potential to its full capacity and promote every positive value while disposing of every negative value.
- We must use our spirituality, our inner strength. We must purify our spirit from confusion and disorientation and develop the ability to discern what direction we need to go, what values and what experiences we need to have. We must establish a set of positive values in our mind and permanently hold them.

This is our inner, protective shield. It is our only chance to avoid being caught in the net of the deteriorating, self-destructive tendencies within our behavior pattern. This is fair. We shouldn't expect to win when our mind, body, and spirit are weak or vulnerable and when we are unable to maintain unity among them.

We need to look deeper into our potential every day. What is still hidden within us? What positive values are still not in the permanent structure of our character? Do we have enough intensity of the vision, enough enlightenment, enough interest in the empowerment established permanently in our impenetrable mental protective shield? Do we have sufficient knowledge of how the whole process works? Do we see the whole picture? Do we understand that this is about our life, health, safety, prosperity, and freedom . . . or about our own destruction if we fail?

Every day we need to take the time to brush off any feelings of apathy, emptiness, anxiety, or depression. We need to refresh our vision, build up more excitement, and remember the point of the game. What are the consequences if we do not create and hold in our mind certain positive values such as inner balance, stability, peace of mind, and harmony within ourselves and with the rest of the world? What are the consequences if we do not hold our inner balance and stability? If we become lazy and fail to pay attention to which direction the game of our life is taking? If we don't pay attention, raise our voice, and act when we see the possibility that we might be hurt by others or abuse ourselves?

When we put these three components in one sharp focus by using the self-therapy of mental training, when we have whole picture of development in our mind, we look on everything with different eyes. And then there is a good chance that we will not only survive, but have optimal physical, mental and spiritual health. We will be in an excellent position to succeed in the game of life.

However, in the long-term life process, there may still be obstacles in our way: temptations, unhealthy desires, greed, unsafe associations or partnerships. These can set us back if we allow the destructive forces hidden behind our confused, disoriented spirit to dictate the game, or process in our life. We need to be aware of that. Just as we exercise our muscles if we find that we are not in optimal shape, we should do more mental exercising at these times. By stretching our brain muscles, extending our mental and spiritual functions, and returning to the basics, we can maintain our peace of mind, inner balance, stability, and harmony within ourselves and with others.

Mental exercise is the key to reconnecting with the inner self. With it, we can stretch our brain muscles and redirect our energy in a more positive direction. We must understand these universal rules of development if we are to be involved in the game of life in a positive way. But we have free choice. We can choose which direction of development we want to pursue.

We can be explorers, uncovering both what is harmful and degrading to our human nature and what helps us and leads us into a positive direction of development. When we are practicing the self-therapeutic techniques of mental exercise, we have better discernment and are able to draw on the power of reflective thinking.

I began to realize this in my youth when I saw injustice. Just as we are able to discern and react to red, yellow, and green traffic lights, I was able to discern a "red" light internally in response to the injustice I saw around me. Everybody has some level of understanding of what irresponsible, abusive, unjust, and criminal behavior is—such as that perpetrated by Hitler, Stalin, and others. Unfortunately, not everybody is willing to do something about it, even if they are witnessing this

17

injustice. Why? Because they are missing the solid foundation provided by moral convictions. And even fewer people search for the inner causes that allow political organizations like heavily armed communist militias or unelected dictatorships to restrict our human rights and keep us in darkness.

Many bad things happened in Czechoslovakia. Personal property and businesses were confiscated. Those who had the courage to raise their voices in opposition against the injustice were jailed. The borders were sealed and the communist regime took away our freedom to travel. They also restricted our freedom of expression and suppressed information. Many people were unable to see the internal red flashing lights, but I, and many others, *did* see them and *did* refuse to accept defeat. Even in my youthful naivety, I knew I had to do something. I had no idea what to do. That would not come until some time later. I had not yet developed the mental and spiritual musculature to know how to act and, at the same time, maintain my internal balance and harmony with the world. It took the ordeal of almost fifteen years in communist prisons for me to learn how to do that.

So I left everything I loved—my parents, my brothers and sister, my native country—and broke through the sealed border to join the resistance in hopes of restoring my country's freedom. Unfortunately, the resistance was so poorly organized and so infiltrated with communist spies that those of us who were willing to sacrifice our lives to defend our country's freedom ended up in harsh communist prisons, as slaves in the Jachymov and Pribram uranium mines.

Only after several years there in the mines and in the high-security fortress prison at Leopoldov did I search for enlightenment and spiritual empowerment. Only then did I seek the secrets to inner stability and strength and the causes of inner weakness and vulnerability.

My survival skills were built by necessity on knowledge gained from my daily mental training. This was my first important step in the exploration and development of my full potential. Even when I was behind the heavy stone prison walls or behind barbed wires in the Jachymov uranium concentration camps, I had wings of freedom in my spirit. I was freer than anyone else.

My next step was to understand the impact of spirituality on the success or failure of my personal and social life. When I was able to put all this together—and believe me it took more than fifteen years of imprisonment to do so—I looked on personal and social conflict with different eyes. I considered spirituality as a fundamental, inseparable part of our human nature. I saw that at the center of our moral conviction should be our spirit. I saw that when the spirit isn't purified, moral conviction is missing in life.

In the eyes of too many people, spirituality is illusive and misunderstood, an uncharted territory. In the eyes to many others, especially those with religious and political convictions, spirituality is something for only the chosen few, creating confusion, intolerance, and frustration, hate, and even wars. In fact, spirituality is an inseparable, important part of human nature. It is a necessary, inseparable part of our basic logic and reasoning, essential to learning, healing, stabilizing the personality, and, ultimately to our entire developmental process. It is necessary if we are to secure lives that are healthy, safe, and prosperous.

Our freedom lies in the three essential components of the self-therapy process: spirituality, mental exercise, and exploring our potential. And by "freedom" I mean the freedom to understand the whole picture of our development, the freedom to reason effectively, and the freedom to engage spirit in our lives. If we build our lives based on the political and religious convictions we have been exposed to before developing personal convictions forged through the development of spiritual clarity, we will not claim our birthright of freedom.

While political, social, and religious convictions abound in great variety, it is only through the development of our own convictions that we can truly be free. And the development of our own convictions requires the rigorous practice of mental and spiritual exercise.

During my years in communist prisons, I was helpless, powerless, and defenseless. I desperately sought those aspects of my potential that were, like my physical body, buried. I desperately sought to understand my own human nature and the role of my spirit in helping me to maintain my physical and mental health, even while in prison. The inconsistencies of the old, formal education system in which I had been raised did not help. It did not prepare me to deal the extreme pressures I had to endure in a harsh, brutal, communist prison.

For a long time, I was unable to avoid confusion and reconnect with my own internal process of development, even when I was trying as hard as possible. It was a constant struggle. But through mental training, I was gradually able to explore my potential, gradually able to accept the internal guidance of my spirit, and gradually able to hold firmly to an important, fundamental set of positive values in my mind. Over time, I expanded my mental and spiritual functions, and that gave me the clarity to see the whole picture and hold my internal balance regardless of the conditions I was in. But more than that, it gave me the vision and spiritual strength to develop my innate leadership abilities, which ultimately guided me safely through many personal and social conflicts.

Not only was my mind clearer, thanks to these practices, but the practices changed my brain chemistry, improving my overall health and strengthening my autoimmune system. I developed more flexibility in my responses to what was around me. My approach became more creative, my choices increased, and I had the energy to stabilize my behavior pattern. I had more power, more determination, and more desire to climb from the internal prison of my own limitations—including the illusions, deceptions, and lies I had held internally.

I ultimately realized that exercising my mind was a very important aspect of my survival in these harsh conditions. By keeping my mind constantly active, I not only improved my chances for staying alive, I improved my chances for staying alive with my humanity intact.

The story of my life is just an honest reminder that we have to be in touch with our internal process, our spiritual power, and that we must use our spirituality for our overall health and safety—for our very survival. My story is a reminder that we need to broaden our view of life and accept the fact that governments, societies, and people can shift directions—and not always in positive ways. And when that happens, we must take a stand. To take that stand in the most positive, peaceful way, we must have clarity of mind and spirit. The processes I learned while in prison, the very processes that helped me survive there, are the same processes that will help us gain that clarity.

Chapter One

Early Years

I was born on October 6th 1930, in the small village of Seloutky, Czechoslovakia, to my parents, Josef and Stefanie Dofek. My father was an entrepreneur who produced fashionable women's clothing. He employed about twenty-four tailors who mostly worked in their homes in many surrounding villages, but a few of the younger tailors worked in a shop in our home. My father carried clothing back and forth in his car, to and from the tailors who worked outside of our shop.

I enjoyed being around these young employees when I was five years old and filled with curiosity. One sunny day, one of these fellows tried to impress others by playing a joke on me. Not thinking of the consequences, he gave me a hammer and sent me to knock on the bee hives we had in our beautiful, big garden. Naturally, I received more bee stings than I could count. For several days, I lay in bed hardly able to recognize anyone. My head and eyes were badly swollen and my body was covered with medicine. The bee hives were gone by the time I could run around again.

Sometimes when the load of clothing did not fill the car, my father would let me travel with him, but that seldom happened. Usually my father had the car overloaded and I had to stay home. One winter day, when the fresh snow covered the whole country in a white blanket, I asked my father if I could accompany him. He answered, "No, not today."

The vision of traveling with him, the adventure of seeing new places and new faces, ignited a splendid idea in my mind. I would hide in the trunk of the car between the clothing and get out when we were far from our house. Then my father could not send me home.

A couple of miles from our home, the car got stuck in the snow when he started uphill. I started pounding on the trunk and calling to my father, "Let me out! I will help you push the car through the snow."

The first thing I saw when he opened the trunk was his wide smile. He laughed when he saw me. After that, I no longer hid in the trunk. He told me I could travel with him whenever there was a little room in the car. It would be all right. But when there was too much of a load, I stayed home hoping I could go along with him the following day. I always respected and loved my father.

From the earliest days of my childhood, I lived in ideal conditions. There was uninterrupted peace and harmony between me, my sister, and my two brothers. We never fought with each other and we never argued with our parents. We had the utmost respect for our parents and for each other. We lived on the first floor of our house and the workshop was on the second floor. The workshop was huge. A dozen young tailors designed and fabricated woman's clothing there. I had all the freedom I wanted when I came home from public school and played with my siblings and other children in the nearby fields and forest.

This peaceful time of my childhood lasted without interruption for years, until I was thirteen. At that time, the German army closed and occupied a public theater where we had been able to see a movie once a week. This was the first time in my life that my peace was interrupted and I reacted strongly to it. It was the first time that I saw the internal flashing red lights that told me something was very wrong. From this first experience, I remained very sensitive to disharmony and injustice and I was always ready to confront it.

I never imagined how long, steep, and difficult, my journey through life would be or how comprehensive my search would be for lasting peace and harmony in my heart and mind and for stability and integrity in my personality. Even today, in my old age, I don't regret going through any experience, any confrontation with the realities of life, because these experiences shaped and cultivated my mind and gave me self-discipline. They taught me how to create the solid foundation of moral conviction and inner strength that have made my personality whole, healthy, and safe.

While some might say that anyone would probably need to go through equally challenging life experiences to achieve this same level of lasting peace and harmony, I believe that the things I learned can be shared so that others can achieve what I did in less time and with less pain than I experienced. I also believe that it is my moral obligation to assist others in this process. My own story is intended to do just that.

Some years later, during the difficult days of World War II (1940-1944), we suffered a tremendous fuel shortage. Gasoline was strictly rationed and my father decided to convert the car from gasoline to wood gas to cover all of his road trips.

No one even owned a car at this time in many surrounding villages. There was no way to transport sick people to the hospital. In Prostejov, a much larger city to the northeast of Seloutky, a carriage pulled by horses transported patients in the traditional manner. In the most serious cases, people would call my father to ask for help in getting them to the hospital. My older brother, Joe, was kept busy cutting wood. We needed only to fill the small boiler on the side of the car with wood and the car would run. Of course, it did not have the same power is it did with gasoline, but it ran.

At the beginning of 1945, the war came ever closer to our small town. Now we also had a shortage of electricity. Sometimes they allowed electricity for only a couple of hours a day. Many people wanted to listen to the foreign news from London at 9:00 p.m., but the commander of the German Army ordered that the electricity be cut at this time to prevent people from hearing the news. He did not want the Czechs to hear that the Germans were losing battles and, in fact, those caught listening to the news from London were sentenced to the concentration camps.

To overcome the shortage of electricity, my father took a tire from the car, put the car on blocks, and ran a generator using belts to produce electricity for the radio during certain hours. In spite of the danger, people for many blocks around surrounded our house every evening to listen to the news from London.

Even at the age of fourteen, I understood the impact of the occupying German army in our country. Tanks, jeeps, and soldiers filled the roads. I knew little of the destructive forces the Germans had unleashed throughout Europe by denying freedom and sovereignty to other nations. They were killing millions in concentration camps and jailing anyone who resisted their regime. But I did know that this foreign element did not belong within our society.

My contacts with the German Army were innocent and filled with curiosity at first. However, I soon had reason to dislike them. They not only had shut down the theater where we had gone to see movies every week, they also occupied the public buildings and playgrounds, using them as army supply depots. We perceived the forbidden, guarded territory of the army arsenal as a challenge. The other boys elected me to trade milk and other food for cigarettes with the soldiers since I spoke the best German. This gave the others time to sneak through the barbed-wire fence and steal some things.

At this point, it was only a game. Afterward, a group of us gathered in the nearby woods with our booty. There were tools, optical instruments for airplanes, ammunition, and lightning rockets. Unfortunately, the lightening rockets lacked the launching tubes to fire them. As usual, along came another inspiration. We managed to weld a cap with a small hole on the end of a piece of pipe and we decided to use a hammer and nail to hit the detonator to fire the lightning rockets. We planned to fire them in the early evening for greater visual impact. What joy filled our hearts as we watched our sparkling rockets in the darkening sky! The spectacle continued to enchant us until we had fired the last one.

Hiding our improvised tools and empty shells, we began walking out of the woods. Within seconds, heavily armed German soldiers with dogs surrounded us. Such a quick reaction by the Germans was un-expected. I persuaded our small group of boys not to panic and to remain outwardly calm, knowing they would be looking for partisan resistance factions, not boys.

The soldiers asked us, "Did you see anyone in the forest?"

Naturally, we had not seen a soul. The smiles on our faces betrayed our confidence and pride but they did nothing to us. We were happy to have exacted this small price for their hurting our beloved nation.

It was unusually quiet on the evening of May 5, 1945. The rumbling of heavy guns stopped. We were on the roof of our house watching the light of the rockets against the dark sky. There was less action than on a usual day. When the news came, it was good. The war had ended.

The next morning, everybody from our small town stood beside the road, welcoming the columns of tired Russian soldiers. Some rode on tanks or on trucks and others simply walked forward towards the unknown. People along the roads were offering everything: food, alcohol, and gentle touches.

Toward the end of the day, a heavy transport of Russian Army vehicles and soldiers stopped at our house for accommodations. The rooms and courtyard were full of soldiers. They left a few days later with every piece of our clothing. Our converted car went too. This was the beginning of communist rule. We were stripped of our belongings. Later we would be stripped of our very freedom.

Chapter Two

Communist Dictatorship

In February 1948, the Communist Party declared dictatorship. The secret police, the StB, sealed the borders to the western world and confiscated all factories and businesses. They simply took the houses and apartments of those who did not actively support their official policies. At that point, the secret police began to prosecute all democratic opposition. My father owned a textile business in the small town of Znojmo, near the border of Austria. Along with many others, he lost his property. Hoping to survive communist dictatorship with a smaller business, he established a gravel company in which only he and my older brother Joe worked.

I disagreed with the communist dictatorship just as I had disagreed with the German occupation. Now other invaders dominated our nation, and I did not have the stomach or cowardice to go along with them. Firing those lightning rockets against the dark sky that spring night a few years earlier had sealed my fate. It marked the beginning of my love for humanity and for the beauty of freedom and prosperity.

The political situation in my country had been very chaotic during the years of German occupation. Before the political situation could crystallize into some basic acknowledgment of national self-determination, the communists forcibly took over. The communist dictatorship drew support from the least ethical group within the community, people who joined the communist militia and, equipped with automatic weapons, who confiscated property. Those who resisted their policies lost their jobs and were forced to dig ditches. Jails began to fill with people trying to escape through the borders. Those who fought back and those loudly expressing their disagreement with the totalitarian regime were imprisoned.

I felt that it was my responsibility to stand up for human rights and do something despite my youth. I was eighteen and attending business school. But it was not business that occupied my mind. Rather, I was concerned with what should be the best way to fight back. Remaining indifferent to the gross injustice was not in my nature. To bow my head, to accept all this as a necessary reality of life and do nothing, was eating at my soul. I vowed to resist until the end. The memory of those who had fought in foreign armies against the Nazis was still fresh in my mind, along with my admiration for them. I dreamed of being one of them, fighting against the Marxists who were occupying my country.

ဆဝဆဝဆဝဆဝ

Now that I am older and have had the benefit of both time and distance, I understand that the deeper purpose of Marxist communist ideology is to help people with government entitlement programs, to share the wealth. Unfortunately, sharing the wealth means taking resources from those who have them—capitalists who have used their creativity and hard work to make something of value and have created job opportunities for others in the process. Unfortunately, it does not help those who become dependent on entitlements in any way. These people just accept the communist ideology, accept better housing and better jobs, without thinking that what the communists have provided they have taken from those who have opposed their twisted materialistic ideology.

This system makes those who buy into it corrupt. They have little sense of or value for justice or spirituality and they become vulnerable because they lose the ability to stand on their own two feet. They lose their independence and their ability to see through—let alone deal with—illusions, deceptions and lies. They become obedient, shallow people without vision and with low standards and few expectations in life. They become the "proletariat," the base of people who support the injustice and cruelty of the regime. Of course, this all fits into the strategy of communist dictatorships: to manipulate and deceive the masses of disoriented people.

We all have the moral obligation to explore and make use of our potential and our spirituality. Our potential is our internal capital— and we must use it wisely, just as we would use our money wisely. We must balance our potential with vision and a clear understanding that we are capable of either evolving or devolving. Then we must take control of our lives. There is no better alternative than a capitalistic approach for prosperity and for our mental and spiritual development.

But it is a mistake to think that those with a Marxist communist ideology are not smart and unable to manipulate the masses. They are clever, sneaky, corrupt, and able to calculate that those with political convictions and those with religious feelings will resist this twisted, materialistic ideology. What helps communist dictatorships is that the role of spirituality is still uncharted territory for many who are missing an understanding of how they must engage their own spirit in their personal development. The communists know that they can conquer these people by restricting personal and spiritual expression, restricting overall freedom, and limiting involvement in social and political establishments. In such a system, educational, economic, and political leadership positions are granted only to those who embrace the ideology. The media is under strict control and the arts are only allowed to the extent that the support the communist ideology.

Forty years of this totalitarian, oppressive regime in my native country made deep dents and created deep shadows within the minds and souls of many citizens. Confused and disoriented, they suffered from moral apathy. These people were left with a shallow knowledge base and became morally indifferent about life.

There is nothing new in what the Marxist communist ideology has been trying to do for almost a hundred years. Throughout history, there have always been those who desired to manipulate and control others. Why? Because this is in our human nature. Within the traditional leadership model, there has always been a desire to have power, as well as material and social privileges. To gain these things, those who wish to manipulate have always given the masses a false sense of justice, stability, and prosperity.

This is nothing new. The only new thing is that each generation produces its own new wave of politicians who make decisions, both good and bad, in their attempt to produce stability and prosperity. Yet, they still fail to understand or have a clear picture of the natural process of development. They are still unable to connect with spirituality as an inseparable part of human nature. And they are still unable to support the natural internal processes of the citizens in a way that produces stability, prosperity, and harmony.

ဆဆဆဆ

My closest friend, Bohus, attended the same classes as me in business school and shared my ideas. Neither of us wanted to be a small wheel in the political machinery of the totalitarian communist dictatorship. We felt it was our right to have any political or religious belief we chose, in spite of our youth. No one in the world had the right to hold us in the big prison that was our country, sealed tightly with barbed-wire fencing. No institution and no political party had the right to terrorize private citizens, to confiscate their property and throw them out of their houses in the middle of the night. How could any political party assign high quality professionals the tasks of digging ditches?

We began searching for opportunities to escape through the tightly sealed borders. By traveling only short distances at any one time, we marked the route for the best way to break through. The whole summer and fall of 1948, we trained for this event. Often camping in the nearby forest, we practiced survival skills by keeping close to the ground, staying a day or two without food, and hiding in the bushes. We had to be prepared when the time came to break out.

With the coming of 1949, the pressure and uncertainty grew day by day. One never knew what could happen the next day. The hordes might pull you out of your bed in the middle of the night and take you to jail. The possibility hung over us constantly. I made my decision to complete the plan. It was time to act. Whenever we set a time, Bohus always had some excuse. In the springtime, the grass was not high enough. In the summertime, he got cold feet and could not make a decision. I understood his feelings. The decision to leave one's family and country did not come easily. You did not know when, or if, you would ever see them again. I understood and decided not to think about it. I loved my parents dearly and knew that this decision might hurt them. My strong determination overcame the feelings of sorrow. Somehow they would come to understand and be proud of their son.

At the end of the summer, I pressured Bohus into making his decision and set the date. If he changed his mind again, there was no other choice than to be on my own, to go myself. And, ultimately, I did go by myself.

It happened this way. When darkness extended its shadow over the Znjomo District, I crawled by myself through the woods and bushes toward the barbed-wire fences. A great feeling of relief swept over me as I slipped through without seeing anyone. Reaching the other side of the fences fulfilled one part of my escape. But I still had to reach Vienna, approximately sixty kilometers from the border. I had not yet passed through the zone controlled by the Russian Army. There was still a good chance they would grab me. I could not use official transportation, such as buses or trains. The Russian Army controlled everything. Lying in the fields and walking in the nearby woods, I finally found the courage to stop a civilian car and ask the driver if he would take me to Vienna. The driver took me to Vienna knowing that he, too, would be jailed if the Russian Army stopped us. He also gave me advice on how to get into the U.S. military zone.

With a light package containing two pairs of socks, two shirts, and a spare suit, I wandered slowly through the streets of this big city. I hoped that I had chosen the correct direction to the U. S. military zone since I really did know where the line should be crossed. Like a blessing from above, a small shop with a Czech name appeared on a street. I stopped and asked the only person there for help. It so happened that he owned the business. Without speaking, he put on his coat, hung the "closed" sign on the door, and led me through the side streets directly to the refugee camp. Exactly twenty-four hours from the time I left my parents and my country, I lay on a bunk bed, breathing a little bit more freely, thinking about the next step.

Traveling by train with a small group of refugees and one guard, I arrived in a small city about two days later. They gave us strict instructions on what to do. There was to be no speaking. We were to blend in with ordinary citizens. We crossed into the U.S. military zone, out of danger and out of the reach of the Russian Army, at the Donau River.

Our final destination was the beautiful city of Salzburg, Austria, at the foot of the Alps. Relaxation was now possible, but not for me. To have turned my back on my country and run away made me feel ashamed. And while I waited patiently for several months for the chance to immigrate to Austria, Canada, South Africa, or another country to start a new existence as a free man, my heart was not really in it. I still felt a responsibility to be involved in returning my country to freedom. My hands were free and my mind was free. I was ready for action.

There were rumors that everything went much more easily from Munich. Immigration and connections with organizations went smoothly and waiting for verification presented no problems. Other Czech refugees, housed in the same room as me, had stolen my only spare suit, my two shirts, and my socks. This hastened my decision to leave Salzburg. With a fellow named Frank, I jumped into a loaded van and returned to Munich. To my surprise, who should I see when we arrived at the refugee camp at Munich but the two thieves who had stolen my clothes. They had already sold my suit. Since I did not have the heart to send them to jail, I simply turned away from them.

During the refugee screening at Munich, the officer sensed my desire to help my fellow citizens. He asked if I had enough courage to do something for my country. Would I fulfill a special assignment? It did not take me two seconds to say yes.

Within a week I was again traveling by train, this time heading for Sumava on the Czech border. I guarded a sealed envelope in my coat, a secret message. When I arrived in Sumava, I took to the woods and bushes. I walked the entire night, believing that there would be less chance of my being captured if I avoided the open fields.

Just before sunrise, I reached the small town of Klatovy. I knocked on the door of the house where I had been directed to deliver the sealed envelope. When the door opened, I stared into automatic weapons held by men hidden there. "You traitor," they said as they kicked my head and body. My ears started ringing and I slipped into unconsciousness. Much later, aroused by some noise, I regained consciousness in a cold isolation cell.

No one spoke to me for three weeks. Each day a uniformed guard handed me a little food through a small hole in the door and then closed the hole again. Then I had another twenty-four hours between four cold walls. At the end of the third week, they handcuffed me, put me in a small car, and took me back to Znojmo. There the secret police began their investigation. They asked every question in the book. Where had I been, from the first day of my escape through the border? Whom had I met? What places did I pass through? I expected more beatings and screaming, but they did not happen.

There I was, at nineteen, in a communist prison cell. I was naïve and unprepared for this experience. I had no knowledge of how to deal with the stress of it. Fortunately, my youth also provided some advantages. I had imagination, vitality, adventurousness, enthusiasm, and a creative mind which, even in this difficult situation, worked overtime. With these qualities, I was able to find a small crack, a small opening into the natural process of life. I knew that the stress of my situation, both the internal and external pressure, could tear me down. I understood that isolation, loneliness, depression, and indifference were the enemy.

I also knew, from a simple law of physics, that any pressure creates a counterpressure. And I came to understand that the same pressure that could tear me down and destroy me could also create a small crack and allow for a buildup of counterpressure. That would give me a fighting chance. Using that counterpressure, I could explore my potential and spirituality, build my moral character, and develop strength and stability—no matter where I was.

What I did not understand, in my youthful naivety, was that this would be a lonely, long-term fight. It would take me a long time to learn how to untangle my own inner workings. It would take a long time to learn how the formation, momentum, and direction of development of my character, personality, and integrity worked. It would take a long time for me to learn that, first, I needed a clear understanding of the process of development. It would take a long time for me to learn that freedom of choice and freedom of expression had to reside within me in order for me to be in a position to resist that which would cause my mental and spiritual energy to flow in a direction counter to my positive development. These understandings were not even in the public arena at that time. I was on my own . . . and would be for a long time.

 හ⧸ හ⧸ හ⧸ හ⧸

Between 1948 and 1979, a despotic, oppressive, and totalitarian communist regime crushed any desire for freedom of expression and disregarded human rights in Czechoslovakia. Why? Because they could. Because the entire society allowed them to. Because there was no moral strength in the society. Because there was no visionary leadership within the political sphere. And with no real leaders, there was no real resistance. We became slaves, hostages, and victims of political oppression because we couldn't defend our freedom. We didn't know how.

The worst crime against humanity that the communists committed was to deny access to the knowledge of how to defend freedom of expression. They understood that freedom of expression and free access to knowledge about spirituality could lead to higher expectations and higher standards of thinking and living. So they took advantage of and exploited the most vulnerable and disoriented people with the lowest of human instincts. They recruited some of these people into the militia and into the elite, secret police, the StB. They terrorized the rest of the nation, keeping everyone uncertain and in fear, knowing that they would be punished or killed if they didn't go along with the thugs.

The communists prosecuted those who opposed them and manipulated the rest into a general ennui, a condition of apathy and moral indifference. And the communists not only denied human rights, they indoctrinated others through the schools and media and at cultural events.

Before the communists forcibly took the reins of government, our nation had four opposition political parties. Not one of them had strong, convincing programs to reinforce moral conviction or encourage the best aspects of human potential in the country's citizens. Neither, for that matter, did any political party in any other country in the world. There was no political ideology to lead nations into respect for peace, stability, harmony, and prosperity. And without moral strength, there was no understanding of why we could not defend our freedom.

Political parties that lack this base of moral conviction are foundationless, built on sand. They do not endure. And while they exist, they are unable to establish and support the conditions that will protect their citizens and maintain freedom. Do they care? Many political leaders only seemed to care about furthering their own careers and maintaining their own lavish, wasteful lifestyles.

At the time of my arrest, a few hundred thousand honest, unprepared people stood in opposition to the communist regime, and we filled up the prisons. During my fifteen years in prisons and the uranium mining concentration camps, I searched my soul and searched for the meaning of my life. I wanted to know who I was. I wanted to untangle the conditions of my personal development. I wanted to untangle and understand the conflicting social situations. I wanted to enjoy my life. I wanted to be free, healthy, safe and happy in my life.

Soon after my arrest, in January 1950, they took me to Brno Jail to wait for the court trail. To my relief, they put me in Common Cell # 31 with twenty other prisoners. My isolation had ended after seventy-five or eighty days. I shared the same cell with a dozen other political prisoners and among them were two other boys of my age, named Lad'a and Milan. Lad'a and Milan were soon my close friends, both having been involved in resistance against communism. We shared everything for many years to come.

There was a special court for what they called antisocial behavior. It happened with unbelievable speed. The judge read the accusations and in the next moment they handed down previously prepared sentences. The communists sentenced me to a maximum security prison for thirteen years. The charge was espionage.

The sentence was no surprise to me or my fellow prisoners. However, we did not believe that anyone sentenced for so many years of jail and hard work would spend all these years in jail. We did not believe that the world would be so tolerant of this gross injustice. We were optimistic and believed that something would happen to help us. Lad'a Vavricek and Milan Sehnal were sentenced a few days after me.

Then, handcuffed and chained together, they put us in a bus and hauled us off to the toughest prison in Czechoslovakia—Bory Plzen. This was the prison where the communist regime placed most political prisoners accused of espionage. It was also the place where they sorted out those who were physically fit to work in uranium mining in the Jachymov and Slavkov territory. My darkest days were ahead of me.

Chapter Three

Bory Plzen

There were more kicks and beatings than food at Bory Plzen. My days at that prison were the most critical days of my life. The book of real life opened for me there. The isolation cell was eight by ten with one small window near the ceiling. One could not look out. They did not allow us to sit or lie down.

Anticommunist proclamations and signatures covered the walls. I did not take time to think. I scratched my name alongside the others with a spoon. In my innocence and naivety, I did not understand why I was being punished when the guards came in and hit my head against the wall. My blood splattered everywhere, covering the walls and my signature. This was my first lesson in practical, real-life experience. My perspective changed forever on that day. I kept asking myself, *Will I always stand ready against their brutality, or will I soon be on my knees begging for mercy?*

The communists had many years of experience with the Siberian concentration camps. They intended to destroy our hearts and souls. Reading and writing were strictly forbidden. A pencil and a piece of paper became our most valued possessions because they could keep our minds active and alive. I yearned to learn other languages, to write a poem, or to study some scientific subject. Almost every English word I learned was written on a piece of toilet paper, hidden by means of an elaborate daily routine that challenged my creative thinking. To escape detection during the guards' daily strip search, I often hid the scrap of paper in unimaginable places. Luck was not always with me. The price of learning the language of freedom was at least three days spent in a dark hole, subjected to beatings and having nothing to eat or drink.

Realizing that my imagination had to be one step ahead, I wrote words in *Azbuka* in hope that the crude, uneducated guards would not understand what was written on the piece of paper. During the years of communist dictatorship from 1948 to 1979, the Russian language was mandatory in all schools. The Russian language uses the Cyrillic alphabet, also called *Azbuka*. This alphabet is very different than the Latin alphabet. When the guards discovered a scrap of paper with writing in *Azbuca* during their daily searches, they were sometimes more tolerant and didn't always send me into the solitary hole. They had probably not learned this alphabet in school and, therefore, could not read what was written on the paper.

Fortunately, I quickly learned the most important lesson of all, the lesson of survival. Survival required constant moral courage. I told myself that there were no situations in life I could not deal with if I used my intuition and moral courage. I focused entirely on my internal state and, in particular, internal stress. I explored its effect it on my state of my mind, and especially on my behavior.

In my mind, I distinguished between values I deemed to be positive, benefiting and nurturing my moral character and those that were negative, coming from the weak, vulnerable, and dark side of my potential. I was able to distinguish which values led to self-destructive behavior. I began mental training, realizing that I had sole responsibility for my thoughts, my actions, and the transformation of my spiritual energy into that which was stable and harmonious.

I began to be in charge of the direction, formation, and destination of my developmental process, even though I didn't fully recognize it yet—and even though I was in prison. I was able to build up a strong sense of direction and enthusiasm. I was able to direct most of my internal energy to my own development during my daily activities. No matter that I was between the four concrete walls of a prison. I was able to put together indicators of positive development. The rules of the spiritual world and the rules of human development began to be clear to me and I was able to formulate a cohesive sense of the entire process.

I effectively used all of this during this very difficult time. I dug and searched the depths of my soul in an attempt to bring into conscious-ness the best qualities I could. I was building my moral and character backbone and the healthy, strong bones and tough muscles to hold it in place. I saw this process as not very different from the way in which the blood circulates through the physical body, bringing health to my physical form. I was circulating healthy mental functioning, bringing health to my spiritual body. Did that activity affect my physical body in a positive way as well? Of course. The brain produced chemicals that improved my overall well-being and improved my autoimmune function.

Whenever I felt uneasy, whenever I felt depressed, empty, bored or in misery, I turned my attention to what was happening in my spiritual body. Where was the circulation of healthy mental functioning blocked? Was my faith in human nature or some other aspect of positive thinking impeded in some way? I understood that just as an accident could block or damage the physical muscles, so could my spiritual muscles be damaged. And just as trigger point work could activate physical healing, so could refreshing my memory with all that was positive activate my spiritual healing.

In my prayers, I asked God for the knowledge—the spiritual bread—to prevent my incarceration from having a deteriorating effect on my soul, my heart, my safety, and my health. I asked for the vision and internal strength to hold on to my trust in my own human nature and in humanity. As a result, I felt happier, safer, and healthier than the prison guards, the citizens who bowed to the Marxist regime, and those in positions of leadership within the communist dictatorship.

My mental and spiritual practices included methods to achieve deep relaxation, as well as methods to recover and refresh my inner energy. These methods gave me self-confidence, stability, integrity, peace of mind, and harmony. Whenever I felt out of harmony, these practices would restore me within twenty-four hours and the burdens of being incarcerated in a brutal communist prison ceased to impact my state of mind. I felt free.

Someone once said that many people's tombstones should read, "Died at thirty. Buried at sixty." I did not want to be one of those people. The whole of everyone's life is a strange adventure. My particular odyssey into the bleak and absurd began at nineteen in a communist prison camp. Yet the years spent in prison were special and the most rewarding in my life.

These were harsh times that tested my mettle and my will to survive. I wanted not only to survive, but to survive with my health, mind, and character intact. How could I be certain that my mind would always be in prime condition? How could I be certain that I would not submit to their brutality through loneliness, self-pity, or a desire to be free and enjoy life? I could not. However, isolation and loneliness provided opportunities to know myself and to recognize that which was of value within me. It also gave me time to think about the qualities I needed to develop.

An ordinary day in prison began with a loud ring at five o'clock in the morning. One could not remain in bed a minute later than five. If one slept or simply rested awhile longer, it meant one or two weeks in isolation with a little food every third day. Shortly after the five o'clock bell, we filed into the basement working area where we spent the day stripping feathers or making "povrisla" (a piece of rope, where on the end we had to attach short peace of wood). Povrisla was used it in agriculture to bind bundles during the harvest. The quota was always set so high that it was nearly impossible to reach. And that meant one-half the food ration for everyone.

No one was allowed to speak during working hours. However, the guard left us occasionally and then the discussion always revolved around some interesting subject. We were also not allowed to speak during our daily exercise period during which we walked in a circle for half an hour. In a careless moment one day, I spoke to my friend. The guards took me to solitary confinement.

When they threw you into a cell, they called you unmentionable names, beat you with clubs, and kicked you all over your body. Two guards, one named Brabec and other one Kramer, were in charge in these beatings. When they left, the heavy metal doors slammed behind them. Whenever a guard knocked on you door, you had to start doing push-ups, which you continued until they knocked twice. It was very painful. After several hundred push-ups, your body could not get up. If you stopped, you were again beaten. During beatings, you covered your head and your face.

You learned to listen after many of beatings. You stopped doing push-ups and saved your energy while the guards knocked on the other doors. You waited patiently until you heard the steps of the guards coming closer to your cell. Then you started doing push-ups again. This could happen at any time, day or night. At night, you had to get up from the ice-cold, wet concrete floor where you were lying without a mattress or blanket.

The most excruciatingly painful experience was hearing your fellow prisoners scream when they were beaten. I learned to start screaming when they began beating me because you were beaten harder if they saw that you were resisting or clenching your teeth. Whenever one of my cell mates or I came back from isolation, the others would try to lift our spirits. Usually they had saved a slice of bread or a bit of food for us.

The time in Bory-Plzen prison did not last too long. I knew that most political prisoners were transferred from Bory-Plzen to Jachymov for uranium mining. I watched some of them come back, lean with heavy chains on their legs. Easily identified by those heavy chains, they were most severely beaten if they attempted to escape and they received an additional ten to fifteen years on their sentences.

I was placed in the Marianske prison camp because I was but nineteen. It was a prison camp for youngsters. Unfortunately, being there did not make my life easier. On the contrary, my life became much harder.

Chapter Four

Marianske and a Camp Called Barbara

The population of the Marianske camp exceeded one thousand. They considered us young rebels and expected trouble from us. The political system and our guards' "politruk" (top political leaders) inspired the most brutal behavior from the prison guards, who were more than ready for us with incredible discipline and very little food. The prisoners in our camp also worked in the uranium mines and faced inconceivable danger in them. The peril was twice as great for those of us who were young prisoners because we had no experience in mining. And there was not even the most basic of training in how to safely mine for uranium.

We lived in simple wooden barracks, the rooms packed with bunk beds. Each of us had an assigned bed. There was no room for the heavy rubber boots, most of them filled with holes. Our poor rubber protective mining clothing hung over the beds. A small space in the middle of the room was reserved for the oven. Wet rubber boots waiting to be dried out always surrounded it. We did not have socks, only pieces of cloth to wrap our feet. The cloths hung over our boots and the odor was horrific. It not only filled the rooms and barracks, but the whole area. This had one great benefit. The guards did not visit or search this filthy, foul smelling place.

The actual working conditions in the mines were the most hazardous of all the dangers we faced. Safe working conditions were not even considered by the guards. They had two goals: to send as much uranium as possible to the Soviet Union and to destroy the health of those digging it out.

Every day, my mind searched busily for a way out of this slavery. Nothing affected my desire to escape, not even the memory of those heavy ankle chains on the prisoners at Bory-Plzen. The all-consuming need to escape never left me. One miserably cold November day, two boys were brutally shot to death by the guards for trying to escape. The guards forced us, row-by-row, to look at the dead boys' bloodstained faces. The punishment was a warning of what would happen to us if we tried the same thing. I took off my hat in respect and was brutally kicked for doing so. Others paid the same homage, knowing what would follow. Some just hardened their hearts. Still, even with the deaths of these boys, my mind continued to dwell on escape.

But there was no possible escape route. We were surrounded by tightly sealed barbed-wire corridors. There were tall watch towers with guards on duty twenty-four hours a day. Between the barbed-wire corridors, fields of white sand prevented anyone from crossing without being spotted from the towers.

In the mine, underground shafts led to dark, unlit corridors. Our working duty required us to drill holes for dynamite. After exploding the charges, we loaded the gravel into small wagons and brought them to the main shaft. Our morale was close to zero and we pretended to work only when the Russian supervisors came to check our progress with Geiger counters. Neither my helper Lad'a nor I cared to help in the buildup of Russian communist imperialism. We suffered as a result with one-half food ration. Our minds remained set on escape. The boys from the neighboring corridors came often to visit. The interesting conversation that passed between us helped us lift our weary spirits.

One day could have been fatal for us. Lad'a and I came to our working place in the morning with two boys from the neighboring corridor. My intuition usually worked overtime. This morning it warned me that all was not well. Other than intuition, there was no explanation for my actions. I sent Lad'a and the boys far back into the mine and began inspecting the condition of our work place. One uranium vein dripped water constantly, but this morning the water was different. By hitting the huge rocks on the sides of the corridor, I began searching for loose stones. Suddenly there was a violent noise and a powerful wind blew dust in my face. The impact blew my carbide lamp away. I found myself in the darkness, hanging on the side of the stone wall. Below me yawned a huge, deep abyss.

I heard calling and screaming when the dust settled. Convinced that I had been swept down with the huge rocks and crushed, Lad'a and the boys were searching for me. Then they saw me on the side of the stone wall, hanging by my fingers with my feet waving in the air. This event did not help our morale. Whatever the risk was, both Lad'a and I decided to escape even if we had the only a slightest chance.

Those prisoners who were suspected of being most likely to attempt an escape worked on the lower mining floors. It was beyond my comprehension that anyone among us could betray another. Yet three months later, I knew that some of our fellow prisoners had betrayed us. I was hung with chains by my wrists from the window bars of the old Catholic cloister called Santa Maria. I had no idea who to suspect of the betrayal.

Back in the mine, I was one of five leaders on the lower mining floors. One day, we made our way to an upper floor closest to the surface. We planned to find a corridor closer to the surface and then dig our way to freedom. It did not happen. Instead, the guards caught us and locked us in small, dark, wet isolation cells. We were beaten and deprived of all but a bit of food for one month. Then they transferred us to Praha-Pankrac. Each of us received an additional sentence of fifteen years of hard labor.

In the early spring of 1953, they relocated me back to Jachymov territory, to a labor concentration camp called Barbara. This was one of a few dozen camps in the harsh Jachymov Territory. Camp Barbara, one of the smallest, housed about five hundred prisoners who worked in the uranium mines. As usual, the rebels, the attempted escapees, and those with the worst discipline records found themselves several hundred meters underground. Slaving in those small, wet corridors with no food in my stomach, carrying a stinking carbide lamp, I was in no mood to help the communist empire expand its nuclear threat.

With all of this misery came a small blessing. My uncle Luis was there. The warm feeling of his embrace more than compensated for the pain of seeing someone from my family in prison. To go from one prison barracks to another was strictly forbidden. It might mean a whole week in solitary if someone reported this infraction. Still, I risked it on many occasions and spent time in a solitary hole for it. But those silent moments spent with my uncle Luis at Barbara were worth it.

Traditionally, the communist celebration days began on May 1st and concluded May 9th. About a dozen of us prominent young rebels always found ourselves in a specially constructed isolation cell behind the barracks close to the command post during this time of celebration. There the guards could watch us and insure that no one would come near and throw a scrap of food. With fewer than two to three square feet allotted to each of us, we could not move. Starving and dirty, we waited for their festivities to end so we could be out of our prison within a prison.

The communists knew no better way of instilling obedience in us. Their torture and terror only built up resistance in equal measure. They would probably have met with more success if they had provided kindness, better conditions, and a chance to learn their programs. These ideas were not in the nature of the Marxist communist ideology. The guards were instructed daily in the methods of hatred and intolerance.

Politruks were the elite ideological leaders of the guards, and each guard was personally accountable to a politruk. They held life and death power over the prisoners. The application of pressure and punishment rested solely with the guards. If a guard displayed tolerance, compassion, or other humane behavior toward a prisoner, his action required an explanation. Criminals were placed on a higher level in the mines once they became informants. The jobs were better and easier with more food and benefits. The benefits included family visits, letters, cigarettes and other favors.

ഇരുഇരുഇരുഇരു

Did forced obedience promote the communist cause? Probably not. The brutal guards and their cruel superiors, the politruks, did not initiate the crimes and sadistic behavior of the specially trained police forces. Well educated government leaders in Prague and their Moscow advisors inspired this conduct.

Methods of holding the whole Czech nation captive behind barbed-wire border fences differed only slightly than those used in the prisons but they obtained a little different result. Most of us political prisoners were able to hold on to human dignity. We supported one another. We maintained our view on life. However, for those in civilian life, human dignity and traditional moral values disintegrated. Our national social maturity died. They intended to bring us to our knees in blind obedience to a group of international communist terrorists and many years of well-organized communist brainwashing slowly poisoned the minds and spirits of our citizens.

Marxist communist ideology reshaped thinking. They persuaded or bribed the intellectuals first, telling them it would benefit them to cooperate. Appealing to their intellectual character, they promised better careers, more desirable housing, and the best schools for their children. Under these circumstances many abandoned their moral-ethical principles and damaged their characters beyond repair. However, there were exceptions. Many highly educated people with stronger ethical character elected to dig ditches. They chose to suffer rather than contribute to the mass madness.

Unfortunately, most people went along with the new government policies, at least on the surface. They sold out in hopes of having a better standard of living. Sometimes in private they presented a different face, but not often. They feared that their children, indoctrinated with the official ideology in school, would report them for speaking against the government. That would be a direct invitation to go to jail. Society seethed with the growing pressure of class intolerance. The police, courts, and government officials of that time gave in to their lowest instincts and shared direct responsibility for terrorizing the nation. They accelerated its deterioration and destroyed the minds and spirits of its people.

Times were hard for everyone in the big prison of our nation and harder yet behind the walls of traditional prisons. The mass hysteria resulting from the terror inflicted by the Czechoslovak Communist Party controlled from Moscow was evident. People from factories, businesses, and agriculture were forced to give evidence against those the Marxist Communist Party labeled "reactionary." Those who resisted giving up their farms and businesses finally gave up. In factories, schools, and collective farms people were forced to send resolutions to courts for antisocial activities. These resolutions strongly supported, even recommended, harsh punishment or even death for those who had the courage to resist. The same treatment applied to those not willing to relinquish their natural human right to freedom of speech, movement, and belief. Involvement in the Communist Party was mandatory. Those who did not support it were blacklisted and in the coming weeks, they were demoted or lost their jobs, their apartments were taken, and the precious opportunity to send their children to college disappeared. Citizens expressing religious beliefs were considered enemies of socialism.

Fear was a bad advisor and, in the long term, oppressive. The requirement for advancement in jobs and careers was membership in the Communist Party. Communist Party members had to attend meetings regularly, and they had to watch their neighbors. For too many people, it was the first step that caused people to break down and lose their inner stability and strength. With freedom outlawed, only the outlaws who overflowed the prisons were free.

Many ordinary citizens who gave up their freedom and human rights fell into moral erosion and deterioration. Those who were willing to be silent and inactive in exchange for career advancement did untold harm to the next generation of Czech youth. The youngsters witnessed the exchange of the self and all beliefs for obedience. This behavior became the norm at this critical time in their development.

Censorship and political indoctrination were the creation of the Czech political leadership emanating from vassals and collaborators serving Moscow's interests. These ruthless cutthroats were chosen to hold important government positions. Some eventually ended up in prison themselves, sent there by fellow communists advancing their careers. These included Svermova, Husak, and Goldstickar. They hung one of them, General Secretary Slansky.

It was evident that even the communist leaders fought among themselves like cats and dogs. To hold a top position in the communist government required unconditional loyalty to Moscow. If Moscow felt a person's loyalty was not strong, that person was accused of desertion and sent to jail or hung.

Unlike the ordinary citizens, my father, my brother Joe, my uncle Luis, and I were unwilling to give up our freedom and human rights. We could not be silent and inactive in exchange for obedience. There could never be an exchange of self and all beliefs for obedience. I paid the price for my actions, as did my father, my uncle Luis, and my idol, my brother Joe.

Chapter Five

Brother Joe

When the communists took over our country's government in 1948, I talked a lot about going abroad to fulfill my dream of fighting communism. I did this at home in front of my parents. No one paid much attention to what I said. No encouragement came my way. On the other hand, they did not discourage me either. Like most young men, I dreamed on, and my parents presumed this dream would disappear with time. Joe had no comment either. At the end of the summer of 1949, he came looking for me after I made my escape. He had escaped as well. We lost touch with one another and he did not learn my fate until much later.

In Czechoslovakia, Joe established a prominent group of Czech citizens who resisted the totalitarian regime. For two more years, he often risked his life sneaking through the border while I swung like a pendulum between the Jachymov uranium mines and tough prisons.

Like most of the resistance groups, the communists penetrated Joe's group with their agents from Vienna or West Germany. People in the resistance groups knew each other. They trusted one another with their lives. Those attempting to organize the resistance from the outside created the most danger. The mistakes and irresponsible actions of the agencies of the United States, English, and French governments caused many Czech people to fall into the hands of the communist secret police.

In the spring of 1951, Joe crossed the border from Vienna headed for Vrbovec, a small town near Znojmo. He headed for the house of Frank Brhel and his wife, members of the citizens' resistance. He made his way carefully, watching closely for the sign showing safety. A dead, black raven hanging over the fence told him to come ahead.

He approached the house under the cover of darkness and climbed over the fence. Then fire from dozens of automatic guns in the hands of secret police broke the silence of the night. Several bullets hit Joe in the stomach and legs. He lost consciousness and fell to the ground. When the firing stopped, one could hear the secret police calling, "Joe, Joe are you there?" The question was met with silence. The secret police found him where he lay unconscious on the ground. They threw him into a car and took him to prison for investigation.

At that time, my father still lived in Znojmo. One night he received an urgent message from a secret police sympathizer. It read: *Ran over the border with your people. The StB has your son, Joe. They have information regarding everyone in your citizens' resistance group.* This happened on the night that Joe was gunned down.

Within a few minutes after he received the message, my father embraced my mother, ran out of the house, and jumped in the car. He quickly drove to pick up my uncle Luis and two other members of the resistance group. They drove close to the forest and stopped when they came near the border of Austria. My father gravely underestimated the powerful organization of the secret police who had watched their every step for a long time. Creeping along very carefully, they almost made it to the border. But at a certain point in the forest, the small group encountered heavy gunfire. My father suffered many bullet wounds.

Some months latter, my mother received a package of bloody clothing belonging to my father and my brother Joe. The package contained no news and no explanation. Soon after that, she received the order to move out of the apartment. The communists confiscated the furniture, cars, gravel company, and heavy trucks. Three other children, my two brothers and sister, were still attending school. Two small rooms in my grandmother's house, hundreds kilometers away, became home for the four of them. The children never finished school after the relocation.

ഇഇഇഇ

Much of this took place while I slaved in the uranium mining camp Nicolay. There the brutal, cynical capo Janicek terrorized fifteen hundred prisoners. Standing time on the counting platform during the rough winter months and hot summers was longer than usual. Green tape identified prisoners who had tried to escape and were serving additional time for that offense. Those of us with green tape on our arms received far less food. We had to work an additional three to four hours after the regular shift in the uranium mines. During this additional time, we cleaned up any sign of grass on the polished white sand fields between the barbed-wire fences. Automatic guns were always aimed at us. Behind these guns, the elite guards showed no signs of sympathy for us. Those sadistic faces were our Czech brothers. Completely indoctrinated with communist ideology, they hated us passionately. The communist society, encountering obstacles in its attempt to gain power over the entire world, blamed the political prisoners for their failure.

Many of the guards were no older than me. I had never seen them before; they had never seen me. From the beginning, I did not understand why someone who had never met me before could display so much hatred towards me. Later I understood how daily meetings with their politruk influenced their thinking.

The uranium mine shaft stood about two kilometers from the barracks. Our daily trip to the mines followed a specific pattern. The guards threw a rope around a group of five prisoners in a row, body-to-body, tightening them into a big bundle. Everyone in this bundle had to start walking on the same foot, right then left. If someone made a mistake while trying to walk, we kicked each other until the line straightened out.

In a political move, the commander of Camp Nicolay, along with the politruk and Janicek, attempted a demonstration for the higher officials in Prague. To prove how well the progressive "rehabilitating" system they were using worked on enemies of the socialistic system, they called on each of us to sign the "socialist agreement." The agreement said that we were willing to work for the government.

They set apart those of us who refused, placing us in special barracks and stripping us of all privileges. Not one of us could write a letter home to our family. Of course, the "privilege" of a full ration of food went first. Assigned to brigade every day meant additional work for three or four hours a day. The unfortunate ones already labeled with green tape became the center of special attention from the guards. About seventy of us who refused to sign the socialist agreement were subjected to daily torture. Not one of us stubborn, hardheaded inmates, who held out blamed the rest of the camp for their decision to sign the agreement.

The seventy of us, quartered in two special barracks, lived with fifteen to twenty people in each room. Usually a criminal leader supervised each room. He enjoyed his position of commanding fifteen or twenty tired and hungry brigades of political prisoners.

They did not know what to do with us. So for several months, they just terrorized us. Finally, someone in a superior position realized that leaving these seventy people together in two barracks would damage the morale of the other prisoners because no one broke down and no one gave up, despite the torture. The one thing they did accomplish was to separate me from my lifelong friend, Lad'a. I went to a different camp—Bytiz.

ဆာဆာဆာဆာ

In the spring of 1953, a special court sentenced Joe to the death penalty. Members of the resistance group received life sentences or long years in jail. Stalin's death occurred at this time, as did that of his puppet president Gotwald. Only then was Joe's sentence changed from death to life in prison.

If one in prison camp can be referred to as "lucky," then I was lucky when I was transferred to Bytiz at the age of twenty-two. There I met up with my older brother Joe.

From our first day together in Bytiz, we wasted not a moment in searching for an opportunity to escape. We knew that going through the barbed-wire fields, passing the guard towers and machine guns, would be suicidal. We decided not to take the risk. We were willing to try other means of escape if we considered the risk to be not too great. If caught, we might be thrown into solitary confinement or placed in underground bunker without food for a period of time. It might be that we would be subjected to physical torture or exposed to uranium radiation. We simply waited for some opportunity.

Then, unexpectedly, the harassment by the guards caused the prisoners to reach a breaking point. The "slaves" simply stopped working. Armed guards with machine guns led a group of us to the front of the command post. They made us stay there, screaming at us, for twenty-four hours. Forbidden to make the slightest move, we could not sit or go to the bathroom. Trying to sit resulted in beatings and isolation. My brother Joe and I stood back-to-back, each supporting the other's weight. Joe then became my closest link to the universe. One might assume that this feeling would be natural, but the close link formed because of our alliance in this fight.

Finally, they began calling names. There was only time for one quick last embrace and a touch from Joe. Then the guards pushed me and fifteen other prisoners towards a specially equipped truck. After one hour of driving, the truck stopped in front of an underground bunker. The guards pushed us into the bunker. Out of several hundred prisoners participating in the strike, they selected us because of our previous bad records.

Chapter Six

Vykmanov

There was not enough room in the bunker for all of us. It had a concrete floor and walls. The ceiling consisted of metal beams covered with tar. The heavy metal doors were windowless and, therefore, allowed no outside light or air. We could hardly make out the contour of the person standing next to us. Half of us rested on the concrete floor while the other half stood. The air was not fit to breathe. Drops of tar leaked from the roof and found a home in our hair and on our clothing. Every third morning, they brought us a little coffee with a crust of brown bread. Showered throughout the day with drops of asphalt from above, we suffered through two weeks in hot summer.

It was pointless to call for a guard or kick the heavy mental doors when somebody fainted. No one ever came. They wanted our complete physical exhaustion and they wanted to damage our health as much as possible without ever touching us.

Safeguarding my mental health demanded constant activity and creativity. I adjusted to any situation by telling myself to stay in control. *Don't be desperate. Don't agonize and allow the misery of the situation to become part of your thinking.* This daily discipline brought me closer to a mental predisposition that allowed me adjust to conflict or pressure before it took place. Approaching my life this way required advanced moral development, anchored in strong spirituality, moral principles, and convictions. Whatever the situation in which I found myself, I knew that whether or not I saw it as an inconvenience, loss, or suffering was my choice.

I did not think too often about the fact that I had lost my outer freedom for my political convictions during the first years of my prison life. I did not meditate about the nature of injustice. Trying to survive kept me too busy. To stay alive and healthy, I had to think positively. I realized that under these circumstances, I had the best chance to achieve the full potential of my development. The extremely high pressure would require the same level of high counter-pressure activity to insure survival. It was essential to remain calm, to absorb and dissolve tension, and to build up the line of self-protection in my mind.

After fourteen days of this treatment, they loaded us into a special bus headed back to Jachymov territory. Chained together and covered with tar and asphalt, we barely recognized each other. We laughed at ourselves and at each other.

We did not mine uranium at the Vykmanov Camp. It was much worse and much more deadly than that. This was a processing plant where each of us would be fully exposed to deadly uranium for years, completely without protection from contamination.

From the bus we went to the counting platform. All prisoners reported there twice daily to be accounted for. Still chained together and holding each other up, this small group of filthy, miserable figures waited on the platform for hours. Finally they began calling out names in groups of two or three prisoners at the time and taking them to their assigned barracks. My name came up last on the list. I wondered what they had prepared for me.

They led me to solitary confinement. I kept asking myself why I had received such special attention. Three days latter I found out. So weak I could not walk, two guards dragged me to the medical station. The door opened and the two guards dragging me stared intently at my face with curiosity and mocking sneers. Inside, I saw my father, lying in the bed. With tears streaming down his cheeks, he looked into my eyes. Standing there with the tar still in my hair and on my face, I could not imagine anything in the world more painful for my loving father than to see me in this condition. My heart writhed in pain as I tried to smile at him.

They assigned me to the barracks whose inhabitants worked in the processing plant on the night shift, in the "death tower." While my father stayed in the medical unit, I shoveled highly radioactive material at night. Thick dust limited visibility to no more than ten or twelve feet. There were no safety measures and no ventilation. It was a death trap. If one could sleep, it had to be done during the day.

Early morning meant counting time on the platform. The guards intentionally made us wait for more than an hour, time after time. Every other morning, a train loaded with radioactive material would leave the camp. That required an additional accounting of all prisoners. We stood for another hour on the counting platform. The night shift was subjected to an additional one or two accountings. I spent two or three hours a day on the counting platform, if luck was with me.

The camp commander kept a sharp eye on me. He gave me an additional assignment: pounding rocks into the ground with a ten-pound sledge hammer. Had my father not been in isolation, I might have refused. I knew I had to stay calm in spite of having to carry out so many senseless, crazy activities. I did what the camp commander wanted, hoping that I would be allowed to spend time with my father when they released him from the medical unit.

As the days passed, each one become more difficult. Finally, exhaustion overcame me. After each morning's accounting, I fell asleep as soon as my head hit the pillow. After the midday counting, the others who worked the graveyard shift slept in their barracks while I hammered away at the rocks. My dream of being reunited with my father never came to pass. They transferred him to a neighboring camp.

Shortly afterward, we were again on the counting platform during a communist celebration. A camp commander came to address us and suddenly start talking about me. He apologized publicly for mistreating me. He gave me a book of communist literature in recognition of my good behavior and hard work. All of this took place in front of four hundred fellow prisoners. For a long time after that, I had to put up with my friends' relentless teasing for being a "socialist pioneer." The commander, intent on rewarding me further, transferred me away from the night shift at the mills to day work. At least the air was a lot cleaner. He never figured out that my short stint of uncharacteristic, exemplary conduct had been the result of my overwhelming desire to see my father again.

My new work place functioned under the supervision of a woman. We nicknamed her Ilsa Koch, after the infamous and sadistic Nazi so feared in the concentration camps. Blond, attractive, and cold, her career had begun two years earlier as the mistress of a Soviet secret agent named Markov. He and his Russian partner established a secret group to help prominent, wealthy Czechs escape the country.

Those of us working in the Vykmanov prison camp knew Maria's "success" story. Her reputation made working around her a chilling experience. Not one of us ever had a kind word for her. The tension build up between Maria and the prisoners. Information passed on to a camp commander through the reports revealed the situation.

One day, Maria Masiar brought an expensive fur into a shop for alternation. Not all businesses in the country had yet been de-privatized. The shop owner recognized the fur as one of his own from the label sewn into the lining. He remembered selling it to a well-known woman from Plzen. Everyone knew this family had fled Czechoslovakia. He doubted that they had left behind such a valuable fur. Suspicious, the furrier called the police. Maria Masiar told the police how the fur came into her possession. She also reported how she came to possess other valuables.

During an unexpected raid on the Makarov home, police discovered a huge cache of money, gold, jewelry, and other treasures belonging to people he had supposedly rescued. As it turned out, he and his partner had not rescued these people at all. They had a specially built car they used to gas their victims. After they stole the victims' belongings, the people were dumped in an abandoned mine shaft. The total number of murders was never determined. The Soviet authorities quickly deported Macarov and his partner back to Moscow. Maria Masiar remained a living legend of terror, a dark cloud over the helpless nation.

Two of my friends and I began to work on an escape plan. Our daily duties included loading barrels of highly radioactive material into a train destined for the Soviet Union. We decided to build a false wall in a railroad car and hide behind it when it left the camp. The plan had a major flaw because the train never left the camp until everyone had been accounted for. The guards found our work on the false wall while searching the train one day. Knowing my work assignment was near the area, suspicion fell on me immediately. They waited until midnight. Then they sized me and dragged me between barbed-wire fences, kicking me all the way.

As with other camps, this camp had three rows of barbed-wire fences around its perimeter. The guards placed me between the two inner rows. Fine, white sand spread around the fences made the area more visible at night. Raking the sand kept it free of grass so that footprints or other traces of escape attempts would be clearly and immediately visible the next morning. They made me stand there for two nights and three days in nothing but my underwear with the guards' machine guns pointed at me from the watchtower. The guards were ordered to shoot me for trying to escape if I moved my hands, sat, or a made the slightest motion. They never had the proof that I had built the beginnings of the false wall. I never admitted knowing anything about it. Nevertheless, after my sixty hour ordeal, I faced another two weeks of solitary confinement.

I wasn't the only family member to attempt escape. My brother Joe was at the Bytiz camp when my father and I were at Vykmanov. He organized an escape with his close friends, Franta Brhel and Joe Cibulka, shortly after our separation. A civilian drove a dump truck full of uranium materials to Vykmanov to be processed on a daily basis. After many days of observation, Joe acted the moment the driver left the truck. He jumped behind the wheel and his two friends got in with him. He hot-wired the truck and rammed it through the guarded gates. The astonished guards did not even begin machine gun fire until Joe and his companions were dozens of meters beyond the gates.

An intensive search began. An alert was sent to a every military group, to all the "special" worker militias, and even to school children, directing them to examine every forest and field. The trio drove about twenty miles and then ran for three days and nights. Several units of soldiers passed by but missed them. Sadly, the next military group discovered them hidden deep into the bushes. The brave escape ended.

I was finally transported from Vykmanov to the country's maximum security prison, Leopoldov. I knew I would be with my brother Joe again because he had been transferred there after his escape attempt. The authorities were wary of putting the two of us in close proximity.

We did not expect to share the same section in prison. The most recalcitrant political, religious, and military leaders found themselves in this prison, the toughest maximum security prison in the country. Prisoners at Leopoldov were completely cut off from the rest of the society and for good reason. These ambitious, tough-minded, career, political, and military leaders represented parties other than the Communist Party. They had organized the underground movements against the totalitarian police state.

Chapter Seven

Leopoldov and Survival

Thousands of people—all ages, all levels of education, and every kind of personality and conviction—were packed into the cold stone cells of the Leopoldov fortress. Joe and I, along with a few hundred other youngsters without political aspirations, were amidst them. We symbolized the vanguard of simple, proud citizens determined not to betray our dignity and individual human qualities. We represented no political party and stood only for ourselves and our personal moral convictions. The ethics of our nation were of uppermost importance to us. Not one of us dreamed of a military career or holding high political office.

Here, against all odds, my survival skills developed further. I developed and practiced mental endurance and readiness to face any conflict, misery, or situation on a daily basis. I held the precise tool of mental predisposition in my mind. More than useful, I found it an essential weapon, not only against my external adversaries, but also against the losses within myself. Thus, every day I won the battle with myself, beating depression, loneliness, and the loss of outer freedom.

Suffering severe pressure became an important incentive to my internal development. Eventually, I won the game.

In the first years of my life in prison, I considered the pressure and resulting stress a game necessary for survival. In later years, the game became a merciless life-and-death struggle. As time passed, I became more determined not to betray my moral convictions, even if I had to pay with my life. I no longer judged anyone by his education, politics, or religion. Instead, I always tried to recognize an individual's moral convictions.

The usual day at Leoplodov fortress followed the same routine for the four thousand and fifteen days I spend there. At five o'clock in the morning, a loud siren went off. Everyone prepared for breakfast, which consisted of a daily bread ration and phony coffee made of anything other than coffee beans. I quickly made my bed in military style with square corners. By evening, I found my neatly made bed, including the straw from the mattress, strewn all over the room. Guards searched daily for any illegal items such as a pencil or a peace of paper. After breakfast, we worked at the same mind numbing routine of stripping feathers or piecing together plastic bags.

I did not allow my mind to wander in fantasy or daydreams about better times, better places, or decent food. My day, every day, began with a simple prayer: Our Father . . . give us this day our daily bread. I actually prayed about spiritual "bread." I searched for the meaning of these words. My daily meditations consisted of keeping my heart warm and loving toward everyone. To love my fellow prisoners, who suffered in quiet dignity, was easy. To love my persecutors, though, was an impossible task. But while I didn't love them, I also didn't hate them. I felt only sorry for them, for their low, immoral character and behavior. Determined not to lower my standards, I openly expressed my thoughts, feelings, and beliefs without animosity or rancor. Nevertheless, try as

I might, I knew I could never love my guards, the communists, or their system of government.

What was between love and hate? Sorrow.

In my daily meditations, I searched for better, deeper human beauty and dignity that contrasted with the stark reality of my day-to-day life. I sought out my fellow prisoners who pursued these same qualities. I insured my own survival by judging each individual, without condemnation, according to a set of private criteria. I could never let my guard down. Ever vigilant, I did not open my heart to anyone without first determining that they shared and practiced the same positive values that I worked so hard to maintain.

Why did I not learn to hate? Because the logical part of me, my reason, recognized the low state of character development in the guards and other communists. I pitied them. They used their minds and abilities negatively, in an evil way. I wanted no part of supporting or contributing to their downhill slide. I even understand why people brought up with good traditional values, might choose their friends according to political or religious beliefs. Great theories and good academic educations did not ensure morality. My survival depended on my ability to read the true value hidden deep in human nature. The sorting out process of people according to their stage of moral development gave me a healthy attitude toward the whole human race based on this knowledge. I developed friendships with simple, honest people who had moral courage. Every day we practiced and exercised the meaning of our simple prayer: *Our Father ... give us this day our spiritual bread.*

When we are enduring the stress of our daily activities, or even when we are praying, we don't usually consider that under the surface of our human nature could be a vulnerable, malnourished, disoriented, soul. We don't consider what is needed to free the soul from the shackles of lethargy and moral indifference. We don't consider what kind of strength and knowledge, emanating from the soul, we must have to deal with life's complexities.

But I was aware of these things. I understood that if one is to rise up and develop a strong internal moral foundation, the first thing one must do is understand and control the flow of internal energy and find the stabilizing point, the divine point. I realized that the pressure, if we let it go unchallenged, could break us and keep us in the big prison of ignorance and lethargy.

And because of my trust in my own human nature, I expected that there was something more effective, something we miss with our traditional view of life. I realized that my prayers had to be connected with my brain and mental functions. I had to challenge, confront, and dispose every deteriorating and self-destructive tendency that came from the weak, vulnerable side of my potential. I had to control my inner balance.

From the words of this simple prayer, finally, came an understanding of the words "integrity," "pride," and "dignity." Prisoners who were unable to find the time to meditate and who were unable to practice their "daily spiritual bread" lived in a dangerous vacuum. Each day we needed to refocus on who we were, where we belonged, and what we should share of the meaning of our lives. It became a constant battle to regenerate and refresh our inner power, but an indifferent life is an empty life.

My fellow prisoners and I lived quiet lives and asked for nothing. We sought no social privileges or political careers. Because we stood up for our moral convictions and rose to the occasion when communism threatened the survival of our society, our lives were filled with inner peace.

The pressure exerted within the walls of Leopoldov defies description. The man who wanted a couple of cigarettes or the married man who desperately wanted to obtain writing privileges to correspond with his family could not be judged by anyone. These men were willing to work exceptionally hard. Sometimes they consented and signed formal agreements supporting the Communist Party programs. All of us were helpless, powerless pawns of a despotic regime trying to destroy our morale, along with our political and religious beliefs. The process somehow enabled the strong to become stronger while some exposed their inner space to fear and apathy until they finally gave up fighting back. Once the despots punctured the inner, stable core of self-protection, it insured a terminal "leak."

Throughout the years of tyrannical pressure, a remarkable and visible crystallization occurred between prisoners of like character. While the remainder of the prison population appeared silent and worn out, a glorious relationship sprang between the several hundred of us still standing tall. The total honesty, depth of feeling, and shared confidences were on a level not approached by most siblings. It is difficult to explain that the years spent between prisons walls were not years of suffering. On the contrary, these years spent between prison walls I would not change for anything in the world. These years were spent belonging to a family of two hundred brave and wise men. We controlled our life processes. No one could change or break us down with any kind of terror. We supported on another. No matter where I was, always some of the closest friends—Tonda Vaculka, Milan Sehnal, my brother Joe, or Boris Achrer—were in quite near contact. We focused straight into the next moment, the next event, the next day.

One critical early winter morning, I came very close to being charged with criminal behavior. My friend Yarda Borecky and I were cleaning up metal shavings in the machine shop. We shivered in our thin prison clothing. An old, cast iron stove stood in the corner of the shop. With no coal or wood to burn, we found one peace of carton paper and a gallon of oil-based paint. Yarda threw the paper into the stove and then threw the entire gallon of paint over it before I could stop him. The result was magnificent. The stove spewed fire that spread to the walls and ceiling. The machine shop was located in an old wooden barrack. There was no way to stop it. I called Yarda over to me and told him I knew of an electrical junction box in the ceiling. So, point by point, we agreed on the story. The fire had started in the junction box. We needed to be in agreement because we knew we would be placed in isolation and once in isolation, they would be happy to label us criminals if our answers were different.

They released us from isolation after several days of investigation and hard questioning, concluding that we had bravely tried to put out the fire. They allowed me to watch the television for the first time in my life. The privilege lasted until my next conflict with my oppressors.

During our "rehabilitation," I admired most of my fellow prisoners in the old military fortress of Leopoldov prison. They rebelled against communism and did not accept any form of the "rehabilitation process." Those who attempted escape from the various labor camps of the Jachymov uranium mines ended up in the maximum security prison—if they were not shot. Only about two percent of the political prisoners came to the conclusion that their actions against the communist regime were unlawful. These exceptions proved to be from factions within the Communist Party—victims of a common rivalry.

The sick-minded communist ideology based on hatred degraded all humans. It presumed people to be primitive, immoral animals and blamed other social classes for society's problems and low standards of living.

The strongest human instinct is self-preservation. It became my constant daily companion. I used it as a challenge to stay alive and to protect my health. I had an advantage over those trying to fulfill their mission of breaking our spirits, resilience, dignity, and health. They did not hesitate to use anything in their cruel repertoire to increase our suffering and attempt to bring us to our knees. As they applied more pressure, my determination to challenge them and stay on the top of the situation become more zealous.

With greater pressure, my filtering system and my self-protection mechanisms grew proportionately. I began to know exactly which values would enhance my mind and spirit and which ones would plummet me into the danger zone into self-destructive tendencies. I cultivated my mind and gained my inner freedom through spiritual balance, stability, and peace of mind. Even in this desperate struggle, I become thankful for my life, although the momentum was uneven at times. I held on to the triumphs and I deeply enjoyed every detail of this developmental process. My flexibility, adaptability, and mental toughness grew, not in spite of my situation, but because of it. The opportunity to overcome my internal prison of anonymity and ignorance was far better in a communist prison than it would have been in normal civilian life. This opportunity was not available to anyone living outside prison walls. Tolerance and understanding of those not sharing my ideas about morality expanded. The goal of supporting life became my daily objective. Once I knew my own identity, it was a simple.

I lived those years of my life with pure inner joy. The screaming admonitions of the violent guards were met with a quiet smile and their cold scorns with sublime peace. Each day, I washed away temptations with my mental exercise practices and deep relaxation. I released and disposed of stress, becoming refreshed and ready to confront the next day's events.

I never felt exhausted or tired while in Leopoldov. The alternative of giving up never occurred to me. Each morning found me refreshed and invigorated, ready to fight again. There was no reason to complain about my role in life. The stress became an essential, positive tool in my personal development. A clear vision of my role and expectations was always uppermost in my mind. The way of life I chose to pursue provided a great deal of happiness and satisfaction. Ironically, there existed within me a strong desire to continue this role. Some might say I had probably reached the state of "nirvana." There was no feeling of spiritual ecstasy, but I achieved contentment, inner harmony, and peace of mind through my actions.

Leopoldov fortress, with its two thousand prisoners, had its share of hardened criminals that included murders and sex offenders, but I never met anyone with a totally evil character. The prison authorities scattered the criminals among the political prisoners with the intention of having them watch us and inform the guards of infractions. Everything was illegal. One could not posses a family photograph. One could not speak against the communists or their government. Owning a pencil or peace of paper was illegal. Fortunately, there was no shortage of toilet paper. Teaching and learning a foreign language, or even having a smile on your face, was reason enough to be punished.

Criminals who turned informers had a better chance for a conditional release. Each of them tried hard to be on the good terms with the guards. Their attempts to damage us appeared unenthusiastic. Most of the time, they displayed respect for us. Some criminals even sensed that their human instincts weren't among the lowest and these had at least some kind of pride and character. After years of being with the criminals, it was common for us political prisoners to know who was a "snitch"— an informant—and who was not. Some of the criminals even kept solidarity with us against the guards and the communist regime.

Periodically, the guards made examples of a few of us by cramming us into an isolation cell with the more brutal, robust, well-fed criminals. It is easy to remain in a common cell with twenty or thirty prisoners of similar mentality and conviction. One could always share opinions, experiences, and friendship with some like-minded person. In isolation, there were approximately fifty square feet to share with a criminal— just the two of you. The criminal made life as difficult as possible every day. They didn't have to discipline their behavior. They only knew the guards' expectations. I had to keep my guard up constantly in isolation with a burly criminal.

Initially, I could not agree with the precept to love everyone. I had to prove to myself that I could talk with what I considered the lowest form of human character. Much latter, I learned that everyone had a spark of good within him. Maybe he loved a sweetheart, his mother, nature, his dog, or his horse. It was necessary to sense this to begin a communication process with one of the criminals and relate my similar feelings and experiences. I would use my imagination to expand his vision and make his days enjoyable. With time, the spark of goodness within become larger no matter how small it had been at first.

During the criminal's harsh and turbulent life, no one paid attention to his upbringing or character. The educational system was (and still is in our present time) inconsistent, failing to teach students how to build a permanent moral character structure. They didn't have any idea how to stabilize behavior. When I was in isolation with some criminal, I focused, intently and constantly, on the small positive qualities. To stir up negative qualities was both counter-productive and dangerous. Admittedly, I developed this communication strategy as a logical way to survive. I did not deceive myself into believing this procedure was entirely benevolent. My mind sharpened, my moral character conviction strengthened, and unexpectedly, I gained faithful friends with each of these encounters.

On a miserable hot summer day, my friend Franta Kohutek and I were digging up grass and raking between the barbed-wire fences. I especially liked Franta for his honesty, straight thinking, and quiet personality. Some of us had noticed that he seemed to have stopped believing that his convictions were worthwhile. It appeared he had lost belief in himself. His life had been much harder than most. He had been behind bars or barbed-wire fences for ten years. He had fought in the resistance against the Nazis and had spent many years in a Nazi concentration camp. The task of keeping his hopes high had become overwhelming. I tried to encourage him. Suddenly, we heard the staccato sounds of machine gun fire. An old farmer, Vaclav Prucha, who was one of us digging up grass between barbed-wire fences, fell dead, in his own blood.

A notorious and hated guard nicknamed Jano Partyzan, screamed down from the watchtower, "I am going to shot all of you!"

There was absolutely no justification for the shooting. The guard's mind had snapped because of his hatred. For two or three days, Jano Partyzan did not appear on the watchtower. However, it did not take too long for this symbol of primitive cruelty and inhumanity to return to his post.

For Franta, this had been too much. He could no longer take the pressure and suffered a complete breakdown. As he screamed, "Murderers!" hysterically, they dragged him into an isolation cell. Captain Vrabel and other guards visited him frequently for several days. Shortly afterward, Franta died. He lies in a small unmarked grave, nameless, behind the walls of Leopoldov prison.

I was naïve and too trusting in my youth, but no one could say there was one ounce of cruelty within me. I never knowingly harmed anyone, nor would I do so. So it follows logically that I presented no danger to anyone—except to the regime with its twisted, inhuman, materialistic communist ideology.

The only word that accurately describes my sentence is unjust. Such a long term in prison deprived me of my youth. However, it instilled within me the first practical rule of survival: discover how to explore and to use everything in the hidden reserves of my potential. From childhood, I'd had faith in human nature and believed that there was much more potential in humans than was traditionally thought. While in prison, I had the chance to discover what that potential was and how to use it in practical ways. I had the chance to stretch my "brain muscles" and expand my responses and vision. I had the chance to build a spiritual filtering system that would discard the negative and support the positive.

Dwelling on all the questions that went through my mind at the beginning of my prison experience could not help me physically, mentally, or spiritually. So I made a commitment to ignore my suffering, loneliness, and the questions regarding fairness and unfairness. My mind focused directly on the future. How could I make the most of the situation and extract from it something positive? Prison life offered nothing in the way of material things. There was no library and there was no way to learn some useful trade. We had only our poor prison clothing and very little food. Consequently, I directed all my energy to learning, following the guiding spiritual light. I exercised my mind, explored my potential, and mastered life's survival skills. Such precious things are not easily learned from classes and books.

When things didn't go my way, I tried to learn from each incident and keep a positive frame of mind. I kept telling myself to stay alive. During periods of my prison life, partly because of pride and partly because of stubbornness, I would challenge the system. Then I would find myself in the isolation cell with a murderer chosen to finish what the guards did not want to do, officially. Provoking the guards or challenging them to fight solved nothing. Obeying all regimens, discipline, and rules of etiquette simplified life. No one ever saw me angry or in a bad mood. Additionally, after several years of strict self-control, no one saw me depressed or disoriented. In the beginning, however, I think the guards would notice some sadness in me. At those times, I fought against the sadness with all my might. I remained someone with a stubborn will that they could neither break nor tear apart. I rarely blew up. It was easy to recognize prisoners in whom the process of breaking down had begun. They lost confidence within themselves and their heads hung low on their chest.

Often I cried inside my soul. I had received no news from my mother for many years. According to a prison standard, I did not deserve any news. It took only one small sign of reconciliation—going along, working harder, or signing some communist document—and I could receive a letter from my family. I could not do it. No matter how painful the consequences, I continued to stand up for my beliefs.

A special politruck, trained by Russian advisors in charge of ideology, once told me, "We know we can't buy you and we can't break you. But you can be sure of one thing. You are going to rot in jail. You will never get out."

Those lightning rockets fired in the spring of 1945 kept my life alive. I came to understand the depth of a whole person's nature, the depth of their moral character development, and I learned how to understand the condition and values of others. Thus, I was able to understand the condition of the lowest human characters. There was no way I could provoke them, shake them up, or wake them spiritually. Further, my attempts at transferring my inner vision, peace, and spirituality to even my closest friends were unsuccessful. It was impossible to infuse another's intellect or character with identity, balance, and the ability to fight in the never ending psychological war called life.

The communist system offered no opportunity to teach or secure an individual's healthy development of mind, body, and spirit. The communists took away the freedom that is the basis for quality of life. Their ideology offered no ideas or methods for developing, exploring, or using or best human qualities or our full human potential. The communists vehemently denied access to any information about spirituality or the internal process of development. Instead, they fostered the lowest human instincts. Nowhere in communist ideology could one find information on suppressing negative thinking. Negative thinking leads to deteriorating and self-destructive tendencies within our behavior patterns. It leads to a destruction of social harmony, stability, security, and prosperity. From my experience, I learned that within every human nature there are qualities of which we are not consciously aware.

Only under extreme stress or an experience similar to my prison experience can the spark, the initial desire, become the determination to learn from real life experience. Although my body was in prison, that spark ignited within me. The communists took my physical freedom, but I realized very quickly that they couldn't take my spiritual freedom.

Unless I allowed them to.

Chapter Eight

Civilian Life

In 1960, there was a big amnesty—except for those of us labeled recalcitrant and uncooperative. The Ministry of Interior played one of its dirty, unique games on me. Three days before the amnesty, guards began rounding up prisoners selected for release. These prisoners would be released on the condition that for many years they would do nothing illegal under the rules of the communist regime. Even a small protest of disagreement with the official communist ideology would be enough to put these people back in prison. These prisoners went to special buildings.

My name appeared on the list. From the moment they placed me in this select group to be released from prison, I knew something had to be wrong. They hated my guts and would not let me escape so easy. Expecting foul play, I did not get my hopes up. The day of the amnesty, at the last possible moment, they led me back to solitary confinement after all the others had been set free.

The malicious game left no psychological scars. I continued to pray and mediate daily, never missing my "daily spiritual bread." I was able to transfer this practice into practical experience. I maintained my internal harmony and kept my dignity intact. Communications with my fellow prisoners helped lift my spirits. The friendships between us were not cosmetic, but shared fellowship.

Another amnesty in 1962 resulted in the release of most of the remaining political prisoners. But my brother Joe, Tonda Vaculka, Boris Achrer, and I were labeled recalcitrant and stayed together in Leopoldov for the next two years. Amnesty passed us by. My father and my uncle Luis obtained their freedom in 1960. Joe and I were finally allowed family visits. I saw and talked to our father one last time before his death in 1962. He died as a direct result of uranium exposure in prison.

Finally, in March of 1964, there were approximately two hundred of us political prisoners remaining in prison at the Leopoldov fortress. We were called in front of judges, one at a time, and released conditionally. We were freed to the big prison of our nation, surrounded by the minefields and the barbed-wire fences, still behind the Iron Curtain. Reminders of the Russian military presence were everywhere. The day following my release, I knocked on my lovely mother's door. Joe showed up, too, exactly a week later.

Adjusting to normal civilian life presented obstacles for which I was not prepared. In prison, a clear distinction existed between those who were fair and honest and the others. In prison, the guards' green uniforms represented the communist regime. Also clearly identifiable were the informants, the "snitches" who spied on us. Roles were visible and obvious. But now I had to deal with ordinary civilian people, with whom I had no contact for more than fifteen years.

I had to be strong against a constant torrent of abuse in prison. On the outside, I had to be content with society's quiet, muddy waters of anonymity and moral indifference. Most of the people I met were uninspired by the communist ideology, but they were also unmotivated by anything else. It seemed that everyone lived in limbo. The long-term trauma had left visible effects on the society.

Imprisonment made me shy and uninterested in the company of loud people. For many years, life consisted of daily meditation and peaceful, quiet times of loneliness. I found it impossible to put down the protective shield and be fully open to everyone and everything. The survival skills developed during my incarceration made me more sensitive to the substance of life that lies within the minds, spirits, and souls of people.

There was no one in the world closer to me than Joe since the time we stood back-to-back on the platform in the Bytiz prison camp. I spend four years recovering physically in the loving care of my mother. The terrible abuse my body endured from constant malnutrition had left me with a very limited choice of food. I could eat very few things. However, my strength was slowly returning. Sister Stephanie and my youngest brother Ludwig were married and lived a considerable distance from us. My brother Milan took me to work with him at the construction company every day. There I trained to become an electrician. Brother Joe drove a truck; Uncle Luis dug ditches.

Joe and I kept the close friendships established with our fellow Leopoldov prisoners. We often traveled to visit them in different parts of the country, considering them part of our extended family. Offering each other support with kind words and understanding, we continued to share our thoughts and memories.

Censorship kept a lid on information in the Czech nation, other than that which supported the official communist doctrine. Children accepted by institutions of higher education were those approved by the Communist Party, their loyalty tested by their materialistic idea of life. Assignment to manual labor became the fate of those not loyal to the party.

Ninety percent of the Czechoslovakian population did not find it necessary to join the communists during all of the years of discrimination. As a result, they functioned as second-class citizens. On the one hand, the Czechs did not want to join them. On the other, they were numb and defenseless. Somehow, they could not organize opposition and assert their rights for political and religious freedom.

Living among them was not an easy task. Under the circumstances of discrimination, with the loss of political and religious freedom, I recognized signs of danger everywhere. From a close observation of the population, my personal analysis led me to describe most of the Czech citizens' attitudes as apathetic and morally indifferent.

The official ideology of the Communist Party, with the full cooperation of the Czech educational system, directed people away from access to knowledge, spirituality, or its meaning. People were also kept from an understanding of how important it was to develop morality and good character. The communist ideology fostered weakness through the educational system. There was a very good reason for this. A morally weak population is easier to manipulate than one that is morally and spiritually strong. The Marxist communist ideology, adopted by the Czech educational system, exemplified a method of mind control and brainwashing that left the country's youth in misery—powerless and defenseless. Unable to keep their personalities and inner strength intact, their youthfulness and idealism quickly changed to cynicism and arrogance. They appeared to age rapidly, in spite of their youth. Their life potential, unexplored and unused, drained out of them and was replaced by aimlessness, disorientation, powerlessness, and self-destructive behavior.

Yet no one could blame them. It took more than fifteen years of tough prison life for me to find my own real identity, fully explore and use my potential, cultivate my mind, and stabilize my behavior.

It took all those years for me to find my spirituality, my place in the world, and my reason for living. Fifteen years of a unique experience taught me to understand my own human nature and be acutely aware that destructive, negative thinking arose from our own dark side.

Gradually, I transitioned from a small view of civilian life to a larger view. While in prison, the woman's world appeared ideal. I wanted to be a part of it. Like any young man, there was a strong need to be a near the tender sex. Not just any woman would do. I had high expectations. There had to be a real attraction, love, and understanding. As a youth, the image of a woman was of beauty, innocence, tenderness, and faithfulness. I was surprised to find this was a fantasy in civilian life.

Returning to civilian life, my first attempt at involvement with a young lady ended in a fiasco. She was the blond, attractive sister of a close friend from Leopoldov prison. Naïve and inexperienced at the age of thirty-four, I poured every emotion into the relationship. I loved her at first sight. Unfortunately, she did not reciprocate. With the door to my feelings completely open, I hoped that she would come to know me better and, given time, change her feelings. Her rejection required a difficult adjustment for me. I finally came to the realization that this wound was self-inflicted. I emerged from this experience sadder and much wiser in the ways of love and romance.

Still recovering from my long years of physical abuse, I now came face-to-face with the shocking realities of civilian life. Finding my place in my country's social environment was more than difficult. I still had trouble adjusting to ordinary people who were unable to share in my level of vision, experience, determination, and understanding of life. Thanks to the flexibility and healing power of my spirit, I bounced back quickly. The scar from my romantic disappointment was almost invisible.

The following year, I met a very special young woman named Atka. She was sweet and attractive. I held back, afraid that our relationship would be in jeopardy if I let her know how much I needed someone close to share my life. My sadness lessened when she was near. When we were together, I felt a compassionate desire to fulfill my vision. I had already learned to experience the depth and fullness of the internal beauty of life. I had already learned the awfulness and misery that accompanies indifference. Now life become even more beautiful for me. We were married in the Castle of Karlstain in the fall of 1966. I felt as if I were in heaven, but I fully realized that I had both feet in the harsh reality of life. I still had a long, difficult way to go if I wanted to share my valuable experience for the benefit of humanity.

I did not even consider sharing what I had learned about character development with any communist official in education, health care, or politics. There was no way I would play the role of a sheep coming to ask the wolf for protection. I wanted nothing to do with anything that would help stabilize the communist regime or help them in attaining a healthier relationship with the ordinary citizens of my nation. Fortunately, I appeared as less than nothing, in their eyes. I was still on the opposite side and always the enemy. I also had no academic credentials that might help me gain access to higher officials within the regime.

Our first son, Bret, come into the world in February of 1967. Helping to bring his innocent little face into the world brought me great happiness. I accepted full responsibility for all of this: my child, my wife, and myself. I did not know how I could protect my family from the dangers of the outside world, but I planned do my best.

Then came the Prague Spring Uprising of 1968. The occupying army, composed of Russians and other Warsaw Pact members, would not reach our town until August, but I was already looking of a way to leave the country. By that time, I had been married for a year and was searching for the way to get my family out from behind the Iron Curtain. The government officials allowed a few people to travel abroad to neighboring countries under very restrictive conditions when the Praque Spring Uprising began.

A shortage of currency required that someone at your destination pay in advance for your trip or vacation. A primary prerequisite was to have a permit from the local communist officials who needed assurance that you would return from your trip. Unfortunately, I knew no one in another country. This did not stop me. I wrote a letter in German, extending an invitation to my family to come for a vacation in Austria. A visiting tourist from neighboring Austria became my helper. I explained to him that our future lives in the free world depended on this letter and I asked him to drop it in the post office in Austria. This time, the luck was on my side. The officials in the construction company where I worked as an electrician granted me permission to leave. They probably did not consider me a serious risk.

To make a final decision to emigrate and leave everything behind took a tremendous amount of courage. There was little or no chance that we would ever see any of our family again. Although the dreams of youth had not completely disappeared, the resources of youth were no longer mine. Now my wife and son were my first concern. No longer would I put myself in a position where I could be an easy target for the merciless, cynical communists. The more I thought about leaving, the more I knew that leaving was the right answer. My lovely young wife Atka supported me.

In August, when the occupying army reached our town, many of us stood at the edge of the road and waved our fists in defiance at the tanks. We cried with pain. Our common hope and the last chance for national freedom were lost. Some of us turned road signs to face the wrong direction to confuse the foreign armies and cost them lost hours on the wrong roads.

Later, I jumped quickly behind the corner of a house when the army fired on unarmed civilians. I discovered a bullet hole in my pants when the firing ceased. On that day began yet another era of grief and tragedy in the history of our poor nation. In silence, we buried the innocent civilian victims.

In July of 1969, the day came when I embraced my brother Joe and my dear mother for the last time. My heart cried out as we turned our backs on the grave of my beloved father. Joe drove us to Prerov, a small town near Prostejov. We did not want to be seen entering an international train at Prostejov. The only items we carried were two small cases and a plastic toy for our son Bret Jr. Any more than two cases would have been cause for suspicion. Maintaining to illusion of a two-week vacation was important.

Feelings of dread swept over me as I left the country where I had been born and the places I loved. I left behind everyone I loved and my real, loyal friends. The three of us had no one close waiting for us as we headed for strange foreign countries. I still felt the last touch of my brother Joe and my mother. In my heart, I did not want to leave. But reason prevailed and I did what had to be done. My mind, disciplined from the long years of training myself in prison, kept wounds from forming. I had not forgotten how to fight back.

Chapter Nine

Emigrating to America

At the beginning of a new era of my life, I left my dear, suffering country behind. I could do little to reverse the suffering of my fellow citizens. I knew that it might take years to break down the sharp edges of anonymity and ignorance that were harming so many of my country's people. The possibility existed that it might never happen. With our son on one side and my wife on the other, I gently held their hands as we stood waiting for the train to pull into the main station at Vienna.

I had the address of my friend, Franta Bim, from the Leopoldov prison safely tucked in my pocket. He lived in an apartment somewhere in the center of downtown Vienna. We dragged the luggage from one bus to another, our two-year-old son carrying his share. We found what we believed was the apartment of my friend. It turned out not to be the correct address. Disappointed and exhausted, we spent our first night in the free world beyond the Iron curtain in a hotel. The next day we met Franta and stayed with him in his apartment for two months.

During this two-month period, we spent much time at the emigration offices, waiting for our time to leave for the United States. My friend from Leopoldov, Mirek Zastera, worked for Radio Free Europe in the United States and would help us when we arrived. Procedures in Europe took an exceptionally long time and nine months would pass before we could leave Europe and begin our new life in the United States.

Still in Austria, Atka and I felt we could no longer impose on my friend Franta. Two months was long enough. Other families waiting to emigrate were living in Traiskirchen, approximately thirty kilometers from Vienna. Traiskirchen was an old military barracks full of dirt and vermin with forty or more families packed and living in one big room. We moved to Traiskirchen. My wife and my son faced each day with grace and smiles. They endured the struggle and never complained. I could not have asked anything better from them.

Four more months passed and more families left for other parts of the world—Canada, Australia, South Africa, and the United States. I could not understand why it was taking so long for my family to be cleared to leave. Several times the U.S. consulate in Vienna put me through the screening process. I assumed that they either did not trust me or they just did not want me in the United States. Perhaps they viewed me as a fundamentally rebellious person.

We later moved from Traiskirchen to Neuhaus, a beautiful place lying in the foothills of the Alps. About one hundred families found a comfortable, temporary home there in a hotel.

My motives for leaving my native country and everyone there I loved could be found in my convictions. I had no chance to share my experiences, my knowledge, or my deep convictions about life, spirituality, and the natural process of moral-character development while in my native country. I did not run from my country to have more butter on my bread. My reasons were more noble. Few political prisoners had the chance to leave and except for my rich experience and my deep moral conviction, I had nothing to offer. Everything was in my head. I had not even had the time to make any documentation or design any examples to back up my theory of overall healthy development.

In 1970, we finally arrived in the United States. We settled in Chicago, living for a couple of months with my friend Mirek Zastera in his apartment. I worked as a maintenance mechanic and electrician in a small company. I gradually tried to put my concepts and understandings of the natural process of development on paper. Whenever I had some thoughts, anytime during the day or evening, I wrote them on a piece of paper.

My responsibility to put food on the table for my family and pay the bills consumed most of my energy. However, my real interest, my passion, was in my sharing what I had learned about human development while in prison. My problem was that no one wanted to listen or share my vision. I could not yet fully articulate or provide the essential details about this process of development. And years of frustration were piling up.

I slowly advanced in my job. I became an electrician at a Chicago hospital. Our material conditions improved. We bought our first small house with a mortgage. My wife and I now had three children. Our first son, Bret, attended public school. Our second son, Rene, and daughter Patty made our family complete. We spent the summer months in a rented cottage by Lake Michigan.

In 1980, we decided to move from Chicago to Denver, so we could be closer to Nature. Being in Denver was not as hard as in the beginning in Chicago. We sold our house in Chicago and bought another in Lakewood, a suburb of Denver. I found a job in another hospital as a mechanic and electrician.

By this time, I had a clearer vision, more documentation, and some schema about moral character development. I also had the chance to talk with some special people—physicians and psychologists—about my experience, about my conviction, and my vision. But whenever I raised my hopes that I had found someone who could help me get my ideas out into the world, those hopes quickly disappeared and any conversation stopped right there. My vision remained but a vision. I had no way to share it with the world.

Chapter Ten

Beginning

W hat constituted an ending for me in 1990 was also a beginning. The hospital at which I worked was undergoing reorganization. At sixty, I'd had hip surgery twice. I took a disability retirement. My dear, faithful wife took over the responsibility for putting food on our family table. I now had plenty of opportunity to do some writing and explore the possibility of convincing administrators in the education system that there was a fundamental need to incorporate practical, teachable lessons about stabilizing the behavior of children and helping them develop a permanent structure of moral-character backbone that would enable them to develop in a healthy and safe way. I still had the strong desire to share my experience and conviction.

I had not written a complete documentation about developmental processes I had learned and used while in prison. I spent the next eight years searching my own experience for clues on what, exactly, had made me mentally tough and able to endure the complexities and pressures of life—both in and out of prison.

I created a few simple examples to help explain what had been effective in helping me understand the impact of spirituality on the internal process of development and, in turn, on health, safety, and prosperity. Then I was able to store these examples permanently in my brain and mental functions. I recognized that when internal balance, stability, harmony, and peace of mind are disturbed, we open ourselves to the deteriorating and self-destructive tendencies within us. At such times, we become susceptible to the long internal slide into stagnancy and the big prison of anonymity and ignorance. Once we have done that, we have lost most of our freedom, even if we are living in a free society.

I was desperately searching my memory for clues to what the formal, traditional system provided me with to deal with situations that lead to that internal slide. Had there been anything in my traditional education that taught me how to deal with pressure, how to understand and confront the causes of that pressure? Had there been anything in my education that revealed the impact of such pressure on spirituality, character, and behavior patterns? Had I learned in school how to deal with the abundance of energy going through my mind and how to use it to explore my potential?

I came to the realization that nothing in the formal educational system had helped me in this regard. I had been on my own with life's harsh realities. While barely out of childhood, I'd had to contend with the complexities and pressures of life under communist dictatorship . . . and then with life in a communist prison. All I'd had was trust in my own human nature—trust that there was something hidden in me, something strong, constructive, bright, beautiful, and meaningful. I had trusted that there was some internal defense mechanism that could help me to confront and overcome any negative thoughts or any negative energy within me and around me. I'd had to find and access this mental and spiritual power, both for my own benefit and to convince others to transcend their deficits and limitation.

In my mental exercising, I had been able to extend my responses and my vision. I had been able to spread the wings of freedom and look at any problem or conflict in life from above. I had come to a clear understanding of the inner causes of negative values and how to prevent them so they do not become a permanent part of the personality.

It had not been easy. But the time in communist prisons had been valuable. It had given me an opportunity to learn how to recover from apathy, misery, depression, and other deteriorative tendencies within myself. And while it had been difficult for me, it was doubly difficult for the ordinary person who lacked access to this knowledge.

The hardships and brutality of prison had actually been a unique opportunity to learn how to explore my full potential, fully express my spirituality, and exercise my mind. I had learned how to map out important connections, predict consequences, and discern where my actions could lead me. I had learned how to prevent falling apart and how to recover when I fell down. I had learned how to bounce back from life's hardships and regain my stability and integrity.

The internal process of development is a very serious, very fundamental matter that impacts the quality of each person's life. To stay indifferent and ignorant is to condemn oneself to a shallow personality and weak character, with low standards, expectations, and an overall low quality of life.

The majority of society—eighty-five percent—have some belief in a higher power, some belief in God. However, it is the communication with the inner self and God that is the weak point. The soul is still hidden somewhere behind the high walls of lethargy and monotony, behind heavy deposits of negative, deteriorating energy that come from the weak, vulnerable side of one's potential.

In prison, I saw many of my honest, brave fellow prisoners praying. They prayed with faith in God and held on to hope. But their prayers were less effective than they might have been because they had not tapped into the power of their own spirit and were unable to make the connection between the words in their prayers and their own hidden spiritual reserves.

This is the exact situation in today's world. Our prayers are not as effective—not as powerful—as they could be, even if we are praying from the depths of our souls. If we do not put the words in our prayers to action and if we do not build a solid inner foundation, we will not have the strength to change anything in our soul or in our relationships with others. We might find ourselves in the big prison of lethargy and unintentional ignorance. And we might stay there indefinitely. No one with a clear mind wants his life to be at odds with his own human nature. No one with a clear mind wants his own complete destruction. Yet it is not unusual to see people internally empty, confused, and disoriented.

My advantage was faith in humanity, a wonderful upbringing, and a deeply rooted belief that all people are basically good and able to live in harmony and peace, both within themselves and with others. In prison, I had begun playing a game with myself. Everything in our potential has two faces, a positive one and a negative one. With this understanding, I practiced inner balance and strengthened my spirit by never allowing negative thoughts to enter my head and stay there for long. This was the only way I could maintain a healthy balance and keep from going insane. What could either kill me or raise me up was under my control. I did not allow events to suffocate me with paralyzing stagnancy and inaction.

I witnessed many my friends dying from excessive uranium radiation and malnutrition, including those closest to me—my brother Joe, my father Joe, and my uncle Luis. I witnessed my dear mother dying from the constant stress and sorrow brought on by the fate of our whole family. Still, I did not allow these events to weaken me or sap my humanity.

The game that the natural process of development was playing with me was fair. I did not have any reason to be depressed or confused, nor did I have reason to complain when I was able to practice the self-therapy of mental exercise. I received more of what I wanted or ever expected. Fifteen years in a communist prison took from me the freedom and mobility of the external world but gave me the exceptional chance for real freedom—that which can only be found within.

I developed a deep relationship with my own soul. I learned how to determine, through deep reflection, what was healthy and what was not. I prayed to God daily for my "spiritual bread." I practiced deep relaxation to dispose of anything negative. Whenever a momentary lapse of depression or hopelessness disturbed my inner peace and threatened to drain my energy into a negative, vulnerable direction, I made a conscious effort to readjust my thinking. When I struggled to regain my equilibrium, my misleading and self-destructive thoughts were rooted out and replaced with focused perspective and purpose.

My new understanding reflected in my judgments regarding others. My relationship with the whole world became simpler. I no longer rejected or hated anyone for not possessing those values I held. I consoled myself with the thought that many had not yet had the opportunity to know themselves or how to steer the course of their own character development.

Years of practicing the inner discipline of concentration, years of following the guiding light of spirituality, allowed me to compete in the field of psychological warfare. I began to notice an inability to hate even the vicious prison guards. My developmental process would not be trapped by these destructive elements. Amazingly, my feelings were under control in any situation. My soul carried no scars. Usually I felt stronger after spending days in a dark hole without food or drink. Everything within me was in harmony and everything in the world was in harmony with me. I was indescribably happy to be part of life and to understand it. There was no need to search for inner peace because it was right there, within me.

These special circumstances of living in a communist prison camp became a unique human laboratory that permitted the best development of my character. There it was possible to observe those exposed to every kind of pressure and injustice. I was able to observe the human fight for survival as nowhere else in the world. In this unique situation, I could sort out the negative, self-destructive qualities from those that were positive and contributed to health and prosperity.

Each day in prison, they cared for my basic needs in a minimal way. There was no need to worry about what to eat, what to wear, or where to sleep. However, the need to confront the ideas in my head and contend with the spiritual struggle occurred constantly. There were no sweet, sorrowful, feelings of love for a girlfriend left behind or worries about my family. My father, brother, and uncle were all somewhere in other concentration camps. Losing them did not tear me apart because they shared my fate. I had a strong confidence in them and I believe they held the same feelings towards me. The burden I carried, my shield, was to not disappoint them. I wanted to stand tall and look them straight in the eye. I prayed for their health and their courage to overcome the difficulties we shared.

Maybe at times I did feel helpless and powerless, but I was close to the exact center of a spiritual balancing process. I understood the actions and values of my friends and enemies. But I could not yet understand or explain in a methodical or scientific fashion the basic principles of this mental process. In my attempt to understand, I constantly engaged myself in a form of intense questioning. I understood that I needed to be able to explain and document my experiences and learning.

There are many political and religious denominations and convictions, but there is only one universal moral conviction. If people have it, there is a deeper ground for understanding the behavior of others and connecting with them. People live in many different environments and many different cultures and hold many different religious and political beliefs. But regardless of their political or religious convictions, if they lack moral convictions, then the differences between their political and religious views and those of others will usually lead them to intolerance, frustration, hate, mass hysteria . . . and, sometimes, war.

But if people have access to the self-therapeutic treatment of mental exercising, their spirituality and a permanent structure of universal moral convictions will be rooted deeply in their minds and behavior. And with that, intolerance and hate will decrease while harmony, stability, and prosperity will increase.

No doctor can help a person maintain optimal health if the person does not understand the natural processes that govern the body, mind, and spirit. Educators are in the same position. They cannot help students develop mentally if the students do not have a clear understanding of the difference between limited, narrow thinking and thinking that is broad and deep. Likewise, political leaders cannot inspire citizens to take social responsibility and live in harmony with one another if the citizens have no understanding of what drives social behavior in positive or negative directions. Even our economy cannot run effectively and smoothly if the workforce has not developed high standards of attitude and performance and cannot even assess what constitutes high and low standards.

Every day can be a new beginning and a new challenge to gain valuable experience when one has these understandings. With mental training, with internal exploration, and with the drive to use one's full potential, we wire our experiences into our brain and mental functions in ways that foster the best—instead of the worst—in us. This requires checking the state of our development on a daily basis and confronting our own weaknesses. It requires assessing our experiences and extracting from them that which will foster our growth and development.

Nothing in our life is free. Happiness is not free. Optimal health is not free. Neither are peace of mind, stability, or integrity. To think that these come without exploring and using the best of our potential is foolishness. We must each do our part, must explore and use our full potential, must build our inner strength, and must direct our mental and spiritual energy in a positive direction. If we are not willing to do those things, then we will pay a heavy price in the resulting personal and societal deterioration.

When I was in prison, I struggled for some time, desperately searching for some way to ease the pressure of my harsh existence. I first focused on exploring and using my potential. It was helpful, but I realized that something was missing. Then I focused on maintaining a positive mindset, regardless of what happened to me and around me. Still, something was missing. I then focused on my own spiritual essence and its impact on my behavior. I finally realized that I had to put all three of these components together to develop the strong internal presence that gave me a solid foundation to move through the world with character and strong moral convictions.

This process took me a lot longer than my fifteen years in communist prisons. It also took the other half of my adult life in my new country, the U.S. I was able not to take the bait of addiction to hate, anger or intolerance and resignation.

I knew that these understandings had not come to me easily and I also knew that they would not come easily to others. Many people, even those with relatively light pressures in their everyday lives, are indifferent to the difference between mindless recitation of prayers and deep connection with spirit, between sloppy thinking and thinking that challenges oneself on a daily basis, between low personal expectations and high values that lead to high standards of behavior. And indifference results, ultimately, in a loss of freedom—both internal and external.

As I have said, freedom is not free.

Fortunately, the knowledge and vision I gained from my experiences in harsh communist prisons can be shared in a relatively short period of time and without the extreme stress of being in prison. My experiences can be shared, but just as I had to earn my internal freedom, so must anyone else. In prison, every new day was full of new challenges, new hopes, new experiences, and new beginnings. The same is true for anyone in this life. But results will come to anyone who tries to break through apathy and exercises his or her spiritual and mental muscles.

Chapter Eleven

Confronting the Educational System

During my many years of living in the free world, in the United States of America, I have had the chance to meet some very interesting people who were well situated socially and politically. I was not afraid to confront them with my vision, with my experience, and with my knowledge. I was not afraid to explain why we need to raise our standards and expectations, and why we must practice the self-therapeutic treatment of mental exercising if we are to raise our quality of life. I had vision, moral conviction, and a desire to help others.

But my thinking was at a higher level than those I would try to inspire. I was unable to convince them, to close the huge gap between us, in the short meetings I had with these people. They were unable to surrender their apathy and emptiness and unwilling to do the hard work on their internal processes. And while I was in the trenches, experiencing life as it is, they seemed to be high above me in some world that was cosmetically perfect—but completely artificial. Still, I didn't give up. Another day for me was a new beginning, a new challenge, and full of new hope.

In 1992, I met a Denver public school administrator, Arnie Langberg. He was a man with an open, creative mind, and he was willing to do some research on the possibility of teaching character development in the Denver public schools. We did some seminars for children between ten and twelve with the help of a young, enthusiastic lawyer, Mike Sabath. We did one seminar a week for four or five months and we saw some signs in the children that what we were doing had meaning for them. However, our attempts to connect with other school districts in Denver and Jefferson counties met with opposition. These school districts decided that to allow our seminars—to open the minds of innocent children, to give them chance to have a balanced view and freedom of expression, to talk about spirituality as an inseparable part of human nature—would violate school regulations. They did not realize that they were actually abusing the human rights of these children—their right to have access to healthy and safe development. The program went no further. People in administration were not interested.

Some years later, Arnie and I attended three day seminars in Aspen for about three hundred educators, administrators, and teachers. We were able to challenge them about not addressing the basic need of moral-character development in our schools. I was not surprised when a group of teachers from Wyoming asked me for some written documentation on this subject. They asked me what practical steps they could take to prevent the high level of student suicide in their schools. I couldn't help them. Everything I knew had come from my experience of surviving fifteen years in communist prisons. I realized that I needed to be better prepared, to translate my knowledge and experience into some practical, teachable approach.

In the spring of 1999, the tragedy at Columbine High School in Englewood, Colorado—only a couple of miles from my home— shocked our entire society. This senseless killing of seventeen innocent people was perpetrated by two morally corrupt teenagers who had no idea how to stabilize their own behavior, attain peace of mind, or achieve harmony with others.

Was anyone asking what the mission of the educational system was?

I felt I had some responsibility, that I hadn't done enough to prevent this kind of senseless tragedy. In all the years of trying to bring moral-character education to schools, I had written at least two dozen letters and I had brief meetings with some officials on both sides of political spectrum. They politely listened to my arguments. Unfortunately, they did not lift a finger to help in any practical way. The concepts were somehow beyond their intellectual ability to comprehend.

I recognized that I had to be in this for the long haul. I had not given up while I was in that communist prison system and I should not give up now—no matter how long it would take. I didn't want to put the blame on ordinary people, preoccupied with the pressures everyday survival. I didn't want to put the blame on the social leaders either, for they had not experienced what I had. But I did believe that those in positions of social and political authority have a responsibility and moral obligation to lead others to a better future.

In confronting the real world, the best chance for survival with optimal mental and spiritual health comes from going deep, knowing more about human nature and understanding our full potential. We live at a critical time. Our children are defenseless and powerless if our schools do not give them the tools they need to fully explore their potential—and those tools include the mental training practices I learned as a political prisoner.

Even while I was in prison, I understood that I was learning important lessons needed to thrive in the world—but missing in our traditional educational system. I was learning the keys to maintaining optimal physical, mental, and spiritual health. In prison, I had no opportunity to share my knowledge and experience. And even when I was finally free and living in the U.S., I was unable to break through the apathy and ignorance of the traditional educational and health care systems to provide these important keys.

For that reason, I began writing about my own story, in hopes that the ordinary people who would find their way to it would have more wisdom and more common sense than many of the government, school, and healthcare officials I had been trying to convince.

One could argue that my learning only came through my own experiences and that for others to gain the knowledge, vision, and inner strength I achieved would require them to go through the same ordeal. But I do not believe that this is so. Knowledge, vision, and experience can be shared and integrated in a much shorter time than I was able to integrate this learning experientially. Some will merely need to be exposed to the concepts, think about them, and begin to practice the kind of self-therapeutic methods of mental training I adopted. This book of my real, personal experience is not about religion or politics. It is about something much more valuable and more basic. It is about sharing powerful, reliable psychological tools to achieve mental and spiritual maturity. Only a fully developed, cultivated mind has the ability and power to coordinate and to regulate the flow of energy. And these methods are teachable.

It took me fifteen years in a communist prison to learn these methods and another forty-five years to be able to articulate them. We have the ability within ourselves to filter and to control what we believe, feel, and experience. We do this through the spirit within, which is an inseparable part of our human nature. This should be most important part of our learning process—in schools and throughout our lives.

Unfortunately, our education system says that spirituality belongs to religion and mental health belongs to health care institutions, shoveling the responsibility from one to the other. Those who suffer from this misguided thinking are our youth, for they are without the basics that will motivate and inspire them to build their lives on a solid foundation, from the ground up.

There is plenty to do if we want to create a world in which humans function optimally and get along with one another. It begins with us— parents, educators, politicians, citizens. It begins by knowing that freedom is not free, by understanding that human nature can be trusted, and by teaching ourselves—and our children—how to exercise our minds and spirits in ways that will allow us to soar.

Are we willing to do that?

ACKNOWLEDGEMENTS

Thanks to my friend and neighbor, R. Frank Falk, Ph.D., Director of Research at The Institute for the Study of Advanced Development. I shared my real life experiences with him and he encouraged me not to give up, but to express myself, my views, and my beliefs in human nature—by writing my autobiography.

Thanks to Melanie Mulhall for her editing skills; I could not imagine finding a better editor to work with.

Thanks to Nick Zelinger, graphic designer, in designing and helping publish this book.

ABOUT THE AUTHOR

Bret Dofek was born October 6, 1930, in the small village of Seloutky, Czechoslovakia, to his parents, Josepf and Stefanie Dofek. His childhood was ideal and worry-free—living and playing with brothers Joe, Milan, Ludvik, and sister Stephanie until 1938, when the Nazis occupied their country. This was his first experience with injustice and he found the courage to do something about it. Even if it was only a small victory: to fire the lightning rockets, to confuse the Nazis army, it fulfilled his soul with a fighting spirit.

When the second World War ended in 1945, his father opened a clothing business in Znojmo. Bret attended business school in Trebic until 1949; then his desire to resist injustice and his fighting spirit drove him to do something more. At this point, he had no real experience, nor any expectations of what it would take, nor the consequences it would produce. He put his life, health, and safety on the line, like thousands of other honest, freedom-loving citizens.

He escaped through the barbed-wired fences to Austria, alone, and in three months, agreed to take some action against the Marxist communist dictatorship to restore freedom to his country. His very first attempt ended before it started, and he found himself in a communist prison. He wasn't alone: many thousands of brave citizens felt the moral obligation to put their lives, health, safety, and their families at risk by resisting the brutal, communist dictatiorship. They sentenced him to thirteen years in prison, in the special political court in Brno. This was the beginning of glorious friendships with other political prisoners, namely, Milan Sehnal, Lois Macek, Tonda Vaculka, and Boris Achrer.

He went through the tough prison of Bory-Plzen, and during the next four years, to different concentration prison camps in the Jachymov and Pribram territory, until he ended up in the rough medieval fortress of

Leopoldov, where he spent an additional fourteen years. Bret and his brother Joe obtained a conditional release from the Leopoldov prison in March of 1964.

He physically recovered, thanks to his dear, caring mother. Bret then met and married his lovely wife, Vlasta. They started a family, and their first son, Bret, was born. Still, he didn't stay resigned, licking his wounds. His fighting spirit remained strong: his gained experience and deeper knowledge about human nature didn't bring him peace of mind. Nor was he willing to share his findings with the oppresive regime, still being behind the larger prison of his nation.

Once again he took a risk and left everything he loved: his country, his mother, his brothers and sister, and his closest friends. He escaped with his wife and two-and-half-year-old son into Austria, into the western, free world and eventually, to America.

Bret and Vlasta Dofek live in Colorado.

Order Form

To order additional copies of this book from the author, via U.S. Mail, please remove or copy this page and return the completed form to:

Bret Dofek • 14420 W. Virginia ~~Ave.~~ *DR'* • Lakewood, CO 80228
303-984-1458 • bretdofek1@yahoo.com

Send to (please print):

_____
Name

_____
Address

_____
City

_____
State   Zip   Country

_____
Email

Unconquerable Soul:
My Thorny Path to Freedom
$14.95 each

U.S. Postal Orders:

$18.95 each (U.S.)
includes $4/copy shipping and handling.

Book Subtotal _____

Shipping:

U.S.: $4 for first book
and $2 for each additional book.

International: $9 for first book
and $5 for each additional book.

Total enclosed with order: _____

Please pay by check or money order, payable to Bret Dofek.